Camping Texas

Camping Texas

A Comprehensive Guide to More Than 200 Campgrounds

Tom Behrens

FALCONGUIDES ®

GUILFORD, CONNECTICUT
HELENA, MONTANA
AN IMPRINT OF THE GLOBE PEQUOT PRESS

FALCONGUIDES®

Project Editor: David Legere
Layout Artist: Maggie Peterson
Maps by Ryan Mitchell © Morris Book Publishing, LLC

Interior photos by Tom Behrens

Library of Congress Cataloging-in-Publication Data is available on file.
ISBN 978-0-7627-4605-7

Printed in the United States of America

10 9 8 7 6 5 4 3 2

Contents

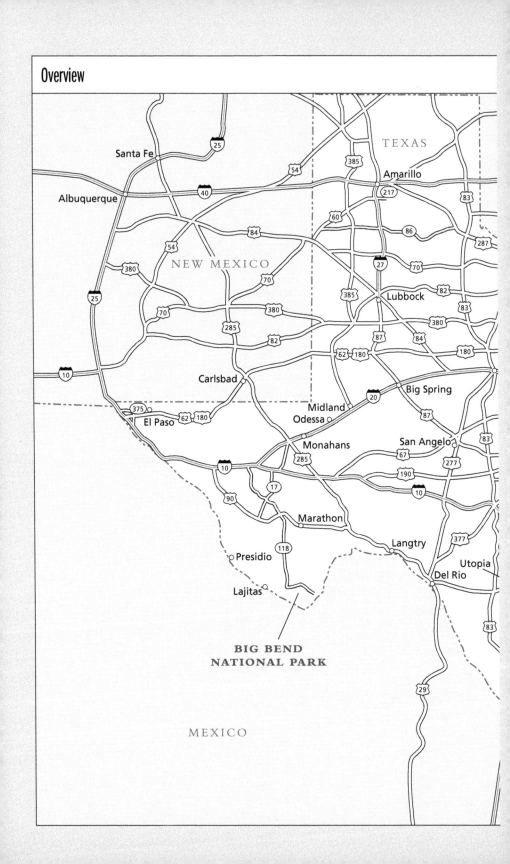

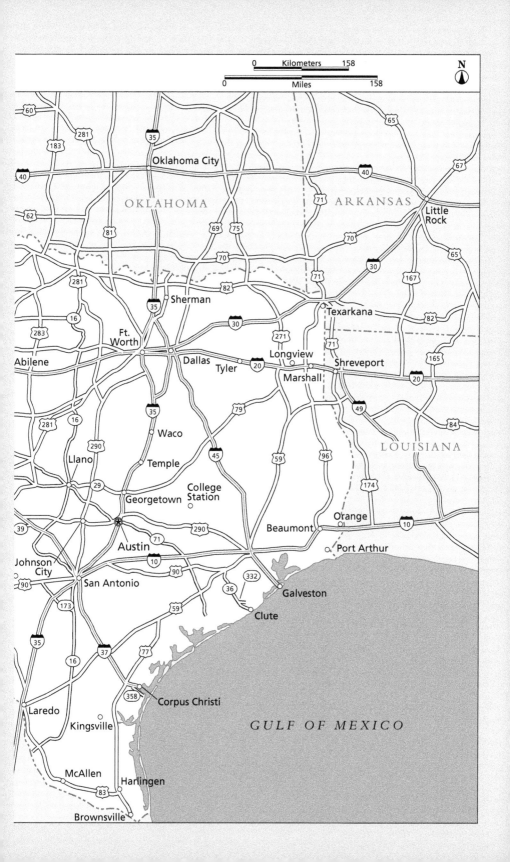

Introduction

Texas, the Lone Star State

As the giant statue of Big Tex says to visitors entering the state fair, "Howdy, partner, welcome to Texas!" Before Alaska entered the Union, Texas was the largest state. With an area of 261,797 square miles and a population of 23,507,783 (based on a 2006 U.S. Census Bureau estimate) in 254 counties, Texas is second largest in both area (behind Alaska) and population (behind California). About half the state's population resides in either the Dallas/Fort Worth or Houston metropolitan areas; however, San Antonio and El Paso are quickly growing.

The geography of Texas spans a wide range of features and time lines. The Rio Grande, Red River, and Sabine River all provide natural state lines. Texas borders Oklahoma on the north, Louisiana and Arkansas to the east, and New Mexico on the west. The Gulf of Mexico and Mexico are our neighbors to the south.

Texas's large size and its location lend itself to several climate zones. In general, the Pineywoods and the Gulf Coast regions have a humid, subtropical climate. The Panhandle Plains and Big Bend regions offer a semi-arid to arid desert, particularly around El Paso. It is not uncommon for the Panhandle Plains to experience below-freezing temperatures and snow in winter, while the South Texas Plains and coastal regions are basking in 70-degree temperatures.

Different regions of Texas experience vastly different precipitation patterns. El Paso averages as little as 7.8 inches of rain per year, while the average annual precipitation is 59 inches in Orange. Maximum temperatures in the summer months range from the 80s in the mountains of west Texas, the Big Bend region, and on Galveston Island in the Gulf Coast region, to around 100 degrees in the Rio Grande Valley and South Texas Plains. Nighttime summer temperatures range from the upper 50s in the west Texas mountains to 80 degrees in Galveston.

According to the Texas Tourism Bureau, the state has seven different regions based on physical attributes and population estimates: Panhandle Plains, Prairies and Lakes, Pineywoods, Gulf Coast, South Texas Plains, Hill Country, and Big Bend Country. Some regions of Texas are associated with the South more than with the Southwest, primarily the Pineywoods, parts of the South Texas Plains, and the Prairies and Lakes. Other regions share more similarities with the Southwest, primarily Big Bend and the southern parts of the Panhandle Plains and South Texas Plains.

About This Book

This book is geared toward the camper looking for places to park an RV, trailer, or tent trailer, or to set up a tent. Many of the different campgrounds listed in the book include group shelters, cabins, and screened enclosures. Cabins and group sites are generally not listed. If this is of interest to you, please use the contact numbers listed for a particular camping location to find out if these extra options exist.

The campsites listed include Texas Parks & Wildlife Department state parks and natural areas, national parks, national forests and grasslands, and selected county and city campgrounds. It does not list the many different commercial RV establishments. The public options range from undeveloped campsites and primitive backpacking sites to campgrounds with just about all the amenities you have in your home, including electricity, water, sewer connections, and/or dump stations for the RVs. Some even have WiFi and cable TV hookups. Restrooms range from none in the backpacking areas to modern facilities with hot showers and flush toilets.

Some of the campgrounds are close to major cities such as Dallas, Fort Worth, Houston, and Waco. However, within those same campgrounds, campers can find remote sites allowing more privacy.

It was important to me in putting this book together to provide more information than just locations to pitch a tent or back in or pull through a recreational vehicle. All of the campgrounds selected present opportunities for some type of outdoor recreational activity, such as hiking, mountain biking, fishing, nature photography, bird-watching, boating, horseback riding, and even hunting in season. Check each location for what is available.

How to Use This Book

The book is divided into Texas's seven travel regions: Panhandle Plains, Prairies and Lakes, Pineywoods, Gulf Coast, South Texas Plains, Hill Country, and Big Bend Country. Each chapter is further broken into sections based on the area covered. For example, in the Pineywoods chapter, there is a section on campgrounds just on Sam Rayburn Reservoir. The purpose is to help campers research specific areas within a region without being overwhelmed with data from all the campgrounds, such as in the Prairies and Lakes.

Each chapter contains a map showing the locations of the region's campgrounds. A brief introduction to the area's camping is provided, along with a table summarizing the type of camping allowed (tent, screened shelter, RV), total number of campsites, and maximum RV length. Most of the campgrounds allowing RVs have no restrictions on RV length and are listed as U (unlimited), though there are few locations that have size restrictions. Make sure you check this column if you are an RV camper. In addition, many of the RV campgrounds do not have hookups, so be sure to check this if it is important to you or if the length of your stay requires these amenities. The availability of toilets (flush or non-flush), showers, drinking water, and dump stations is also indicated along with the outdoor recreation available at each campground.

The last column gives an indication of the campsite rental cost per night ($ = less than $10, $$ = $10 to $19, $$$ = $20 or more). Please note that at some campgrounds, a campground entrance fee or boat launch fee may be charged in addition to the camping fee. If there is an additional fee, most often it is part of the camping fee.

Key:

Hookups:

W	–	Water
E	–	Electric
S	–	Sewer
C	–	Cable
P	–	Phone
I	–	Internet

Campsites:

T	–	Tents
S	–	Screened shelters
R	–	Recreational vehicles

Max RV Length: Given in feet;

U	–	No length restrictions

Toilets:

F	–	Flush
NF	–	No flush

Recreation:

H	–	Hiking
S	–	Swimming
F	–	Fishing
B	–	Boating
L	–	Boat launch
R	–	Horseback riding
C	–	Cycling and mountain biking
J	–	Canoe/johnboat rentals

The price range is as follows:

$	=	$10 or less
$$	=	$11–19
$$$	=	$20 and higher

Every campground has an "About the campground" section that gives additional useful information about the campground and surrounding area. Make sure you use the "Contact" phone number before going to any campground. In Texas, heavy rains, flooding, drought, hurricanes, wildfires, etc., may cause campgrounds to shut down. Location, entrance fees (if any), season, number of camping sites, length restrictions on RVs (if any), facilities available, camping site fees, management, contact phone numbers, and information of how to find the campground is given. Additional information, such as guide service, dry and wet storage for boats, etc. may be listed for each different campground.

Campground Passes and Passports

The Texas State Parks Pass is an annual pass that offers many special benefits. As a member, you and your guests can enjoy unlimited visits to state parks, state historic sites, and state natural areas without paying the daily entrance fee. Members also receive discounts on camping, Texas State Park Store merchandise, and recreational equipment rentals, and are eligible for special promotions like waived activity fees and free programs.

The National Parks and Federal Lands Recreational Pass is valid for one full year from the month of purchase. This pass provides entrance or access to the pass holder and accompanying passengers at federally operated recreation sites across the country.

Fees and policies vary widely across the thousands of federal recreation sites, so please contact specific sites directly for information on what is or is not covered. If you are 62 or older or receive disability benefits, you may be eligible for the Senior or Access pass.

The Texas State Parks Pass is available at most state parks and historic sites, as well as through the Customer Service Center in Austin, Texas (512-389-8900).

Zero Impact

Probably the most valuable thing for humans and nature is observing a zero-impact backcountry ethic. Exercise these simple rules and you'll get along fine in any campground in Texas. The following is a simplified version pertaining to campgrounds.

Plan ahead and prepare: Research your campground and its regulations. Purchase the maps, permits, and supplies you need for each campground. In case of emergency, pack survival gear.

Minimize impact: Camp within the designated camping areas on durable surfaces. Use the established sites and do not stray out of established tent pads and parking spaces. The same goes for footpaths or hiking trails. Even if a footpath is wet or muddy, walk through it. Stepping off the trail damages the surrounding vegetation and widens your impact. Use the designated fire pits. If the area is open to fires, use a pit that has already been established. Collect dead wood and keep your fire small.

Dispose of your waste: Dispose of all your trash properly. If there are no garbage cans at the campground, pack out your waste with you. The same goes for any garbage you may have found left by others. Bring sealed containers and bags for packing all materials out. Never leave behind or bury anything. Do not put garbage in vault toilets. Remove all unburned materials from your fire ring.

Leave what you find: Collecting materials of any kind at most campgrounds is illegal. Always check the regulations before you collect firewood.

Respect wildlife: Never disturb or inhibit an animal you encounter. Observe these creatures from a distance; do not stalk them for photos. Do not interfere with their activities. *Never* feed the animals.

Respect neighbors: Keep your camp quiet. Keep your voices low and leave stereos at home. Enjoy the soft sounds of nature and minimize the effect of your presence.

Big skies, gorgeous sunsets, and breathtaking vistas characterize the Panhandle Plains of north Texas. *Travel Texas* boasts that the stars at night are big and bright in the Panhandle Plains. With its wide-open spaces and rolling plains, this region boasts some of the clearest and brightest star-filled evening skies you'll find anywhere in the Lone Star State, and that's just the beginning.

Rugged beauty is all around visitors in this area, from the vast expanses of fertile farmland to the water-carved canyons and scenic lakes. Twenty-six campgrounds offer camping experiences for everyone from the RV camper to the primitive backpacker. Saddle up your horse, or rent one at some of the campgrounds, and experience what some of the earliest people of Texas felt as they made their way across the state, some heading farther west.

The Panhandle Plains stretch from the Texas-Oklahoma border south to San Angelo. New Mexico borders on the west. Wichita Falls and Brownwood are anchor cities along the eastern border, while the northern part of the region is dominated by Amarillo. Other historic Texas cities and towns within this geographical area are Lubbock and Abilene.

Just to the south of San Angelo lies one of the state's most beautiful natural attractions, Palo Duro Canyon State Park in Canyon. One of the largest state parks in Texas, it features more than 18,000 acres of majestic scenery, including walls that plunge nearly 1,000 feet to the canyon floor.

A portion of the historic official Texas longhorn herd resides in Fort Griffin State Park and Historic Site. Comanche and other Indian tribes roamed these rolling plains. Caprock Canyons State Park's lengthy Trailway is open for hiking, biking, and equestrian use. Recreational adventure stretches from the western terminus at the South Plains on top of the caprock escarpment to the eastern terminus of Estelline in the Red River Valley.

Campers in the Panhandle Plains have a wide assortment of outdoor adventures from which to choose. From fishing, boating, hiking, and swimming to nature study, photography, and historic sites, it's all here for the taking at the different campgrounds in this region.

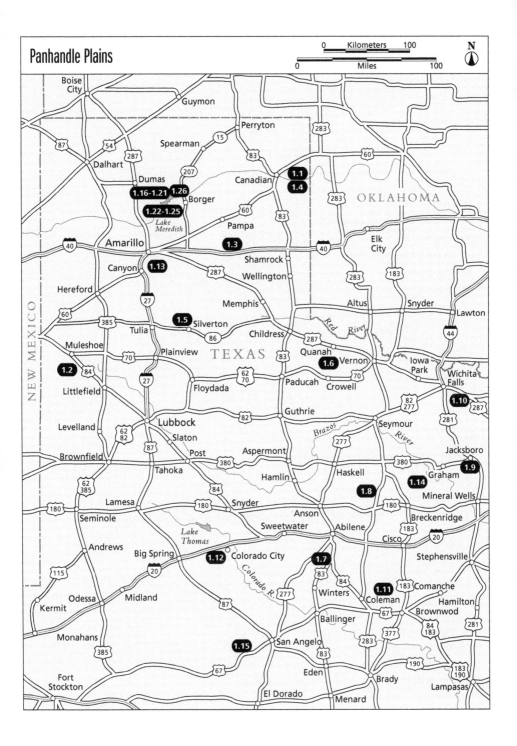

Panhandle Plains

0 Kilometers 100

0 Miles 100

N

Boise City
Guymon
Perryton
283
Spearman
15
87
54
287
83
60
Dalhart
207
Dumas
Canadian
1.1
1.16-1.21 **1.26**
1.4
Borger
283
OKLAHOMA
1.22-1.25
60
83
Lake Meredith
Pampa
Elk City
40
Amarillo
1.3
40
Canyon **1.13**
Shamrock
287
Wellington
283
183
Hereford
27
Memphis
Altus
Snyder
60
385
1.5 Silverton
Lawton
Tulia
86
Childress
287
Red River
44
Muleshoe
Plainview
T E X A S
83
Quanah
1.2 84
27
Floydada
62 70
Paducah
Vernon **1.6**
70
Crowell
Iowa Park
Wichita Falls
Littlefield
82
Guthrie
Brazos River
82 277
1.10
Levelland
Lubbock
62 82
Slaton
Seymour
281
287
Brownfield
87
Post
Aspermont
277
380
Jacksboro
Tahoka
380
Graham **1.9**
84
Hamlin
Haskell
1.14
Mineral Wells
Lamesa
180
Snyder
1.8
180
Seminole
Anson
Breckenridge
180
180
Sweetwater
Abilene
183
Andrews
Lake Thomas
Cisco
20
Big Spring
1.12 Colorado City
1.7
Stephensville
115
20
Colorado R.
83
Comanche
Odessa
Midland
277
84
183
Kermit
87
Winters
Coleman **1.11**
Hamilton
Brownwod
Monahans
Ballinger
67
84 183
281
385
1.15 San Angelo
377
283
Fort Stockton
67
83
190
183 190
Eden
Brady
Lampasas
El Dorado
Menard

Panhandle Plains

	Campsites	Total Sites	Max RV Length	Hookups	Toilets	Showers	Drinking Water	Dump Station	Recreation	Fee
1.1 Gene Howe WMA	TR	7	U		NF				H	$$
1.2 Muleshoe NWR	TR	*	U		NF		X		H	
1.3 McClellan Creek National Grasslands RA	TR	40	U	EW	F	X	X	X	HF	$$
1.4 Lake Marvin RA	TR	15	U	EW	NF		X		HFL	$$
1.5 Caprock Canyons SP & Trailway	TR	136	U	EW	F, NF	X	X	X	HSFBLRC	$-$$$
1.6 Copper Breaks SP	TR	52	U	EW	F, NF	X	X	X	HSFBLRC	$-$$$
1.7 Abilene SP	TR	94	U	EWS	F, NF	X	X	X	HSFC	$-$$
1.8 Fort Griffin SP	TR	28	U	EWS	F, NF	X	X	X	HRF	$$-$$$
1.9 Fort Richardson SP	TRS	73	U	EWS	F, NF	X	X	X	HSFRC	$-$$
1.10 Lake Arrowhead SP	TR	76	U	EW	F, NF	X	X	X	HFBLR	$-$$$
1.11 Lake Brownwood SP	TR	87	U	EWS	F, NF	X	X	X	HSFB	$$-$$$
1.12 Lake Colorado City SP	TR	112	U	EW	F, NF	X	X	X	HSFB	$$-$$$
1.13 Palo Duro Canyon SP	TR	114	50	EW	F, NF	X	X	X	HRC	$$-$$$
1.14 Possum Kingdom SP	TR	136	U	EW	F, NF	X	X	X	HSFBLC	$-$$$
1.15 San Angelo SP	TR	277	U	EW	F, NF	X	X	X	HSFBRC	$-$$

* No defined information on the number of campsites

1.1   Gene Howe Wildlife Management Area

Location: Canadian
Entrance fee: Limited Public Use permit required
Season: Open year-round, except during special hunting seasons (contact the WMA for current park status)
Camping sites: 7 primitive sites
Maximum length: No length restrictions
Facilities: Fire rings, composting toilets, no drinking water
Fees per night: $$
Management: Texas Parks & Wildlife Department
Contact: (806) 323-8642

Finding the campground: From Canadian, heading north on US 83/US 60, turn right (east) on FM 2266 and go about 6 miles to the registration and information station.

About the campground: The Gene Howe Wildlife Management Area (GHWMA) contains 5,886 acres located along the Canadian River in the northern rolling plains of Hemphill County, about 7 miles north of the town of Canadian. It is composed of roughly two-thirds sand sage/midgrass rangeland and one-third cottonwood/tallgrass bottomland. Numerous wildlife species can be found in the GHWMA, both small and big game. Designated public hunting roads enter the various sections, allowing visitors to reach interior undisturbed environment. Some areas in the GHWMA are inaccessible to two-wheel-drive vehicles; therefore, four-wheel drive is recommended to gain access to these areas. Due to high water levels during the winter, some of the bottomlands are not accessible even with a four-wheel drive. Users may not camp or build a fire anywhere in the GHWMA other than in designated campsites, and the cutting of firewood is prohibited.

1.2   Muleshoe National Wildlife Refuge

Location: 20 miles south of Muleshoe
Entrance fee: None
Season: Open year-round
Camping sites: A camping area is located near the refuge headquarters with numerous primitive camping sites available. No hookups are available. A central water source is available, along with restrooms.
Maximum length: No length restrictions
Facilities: Fire pits, grills, picnic tables, drinking water, pit toilets
Fees per night: None
Management: U.S. Fish & Wildlife Service
Contact: (806) 946-3341
Finding the campground: From Muleshoe, take TX 214 south 20 miles, then go west on Caliche Road for 2.25 miles to refuge headquarters.
About the campground: Muleshoe (5,809 acres) is the oldest national wildlife refuge in Texas and is one of a chain of refuges in the Central Flyway. Located on the high plains of west Texas, Muleshoe was established as a wintering area for migratory waterfowl and sandhill cranes. When sufficient water is present, the refuge hosts large numbers of sandhill cranes and a variety of other waterfowl. Muleshoe has three sink-type lakes that have no outlets and depend entirely on runoff for water, so they are periodically dry. When the lakes are full, 600 acres of water are available for wildlife. Visitors are welcome to travel the refuge roads during daylight hours. A visitor center in the refuge office displays some mounted birds and mammals common to the area. A picnic area and 1-mile nature trail is located near the refuge headquarters, and a 0.25-mile nature trail is at Paul's Lake, 6 miles northeast of the headquarters.

1.3 McClellan Creek National Grasslands Recreation Area

Location: 3 miles north of I-40 exit 128, near Pampa
Entrance fee: Day-use fee
Season: Open year-round
Camping sites: Northwest side of lake has 17 sites with electric and water hookups, 16 sites without hookups; southeast side has 7 sites with no hookups
Maximum length: No length restrictions
Facilities: Restrooms with showers, drinking water, picnic area, dump station on northwest side of the lake
Fees per night: $$
Management: USDA Forest Service
Contact: (580) 497-2143
Finding the campground: From I-40, exit 128, go 3 miles north on Hwy 2477 to McClellan Creek Recreation Area.
About the campground: McClellan Creek Recreation Area contains 1,449 acres near Pampa in Gray County. Lake McClellan offers picnicking, fishing, and wildlife-viewing opportunities year-round. Hiking trails are available at most areas, and all have access for cross-county travel on undeveloped portions of the grasslands.

1.4 Lake Marvin Recreation Area

Location: 12 miles east of Canadian
Entrance fee: None
Season: Open year-round
Camping sites: 15 sites, 6 with water and electric hookups; 15 without hookups
Maximum length: No length restrictions
Facilities: Pit toilets, drinking water, picnic area
Fees per night: $$
Management: USDA Forest Service
Contact: (580) 497-2143
Finding the campground: From Canadian, go 12 miles east on FM 2266.
About the campground: Hiking trails are available, along with a 40-acre fishing lake with small boat ramp. The Big Tree Trail was used as a reference point for wagon trains going west.

1.5   Caprock Canyons State Park and Trailway

Location: Quitaque
Entrance fee: Small fee
Season: Open year-round
Camping sites: 40 backpacking sites in North Prong and South Prong areas; 40 developed walk-in tent sites in South Prong and Little Red areas; 12 developed equestrian sites (non-equestrian camping is allowed); 9 sites with water in Lake Theo area; 35 sites with water and either 30-amp (25 sites) or 50-amp (10 sites) electric hookups in Honey Flat area; primitive camping along length of Trailway
Maximum length: No length restrictions
Facilities: Restrooms, showers, dump station; North Prong and South Prong have organic restrooms and 16.3 miles of associated trails; equestrian sites have corrals, tables, grills, water for horses, and parking at individual sites; Lake Theo has picnic tables, fire rings, and lantern posts; Honey Flat has shade shelters, picnic tables, fire rings, and lantern posts
Fees per night: $-$$$
Contact: (806) 455-1492
Finding the campground: The park is 3.5 miles north of Quitaque on FM 1065 in Quitaque.
About the campground: Caprock Canyons State Park, 100 miles southeast of Amarillo in Briscoe County, opened in 1982. It consists of 15,314 acres, including the Trailway, a 64.25-mile rail-to-trail conversion, acquired by donation in 1992 from a railroad entrepreneur. This acquisition added recreational adventure stretching from the western terminus at the South Plains on top of the caprock escarpment to the eastern terminus of Estelline in the Red River Valley. There are almost 90 miles of multiuse trails ranging from the very difficult in rugged terrain to those with less than 3 percent grade. About 25 miles include cliffs and drop-offs, with steep climbs and descents that are recommended only for the experienced equestrian and mountain biker. Water is usually available for animals along the trails and some potable water is available at selected sites, but it is highly recommended that personal water is carried for each adventurer.

In addition to hiking, horseback riding, and mountain biking, the park offers boating on a no-wake lake (120 surface acres, 30 feet deep when full) with boat ramp, a scenic drive, guided tours, interpretive exhibits, a fishing pier, a swimming beach, a Texas State Park Store, and seasonal concessions offering horse rentals.

1.6   Copper Breaks State Park

Location: Between Quanah and Crowell
Entrance fee: Small fee
Season: Open year-round
Camping sites: 25 sites with 50-amp electric and water hookups; 11 sites with water; 10 equestrian sites with water; 6 hike-in (0.75 mile) primitive sites
Maximum length: No length restrictions
Facilities: Restrooms with and without showers, dump station, group picnic pavilion with adjacent group picnic area; equestrian area has two 5-foot tying rails
Fees per night: $-$$$
Management: Texas Parks & Wildlife Department
Contact: (940) 839-4331
Finding the campground: The park is located 12 miles from Quanah and 8 miles from Crowell on TX 6. Enter the park on Park Road 62.
About the campground: A portion of the official Texas longhorn herd is maintained at the park. Activities include picnicking, mountain biking, wildlife viewing, backpacking, kite flying, horseback riding (horse rentals not available), summer educational and interpretive programs, playgrounds, and natural and historical exhibits. Two lakes (60 acres and 10 acres) offer swimming, boating (ramp and dock), and fishing (pier). There are 9.5 miles of trail for backpacking, mountain biking, and horseback riding over varying terrain, along with a 0.5-mile nature trail. All 10 miles may be used for day hiking.

1.7   Abilene State Park

Location: Tuscola
Entrance fee: Small fee
Season: Open year-round
Camping sites: 35 sites with electric and water hookups in the Group Trailer Area; 41 sites with electric and water hookups; 3 sites with electric, water, and sewer hookup; 12 tent-only sites with water; 3 tent-only sites without water
Maximum length: No length restrictions
Facilities: Restrooms with and without showers, RV dump station
Fees per night: $-$$
Management: Texas Parks & Wildlife Department
Contact: (325) 572-3204
Finding the campground: From Abilene, travel 16 miles southwest on FM 89, through Buffalo Gap, then on Park Road 32 to the park entrance.
About the campground: Abilene State Park offers camping, hiking, nature study, picnicking, fishing in the park's Buffalo Wallow Pond and nearby Lake Abilene, and biking and walking on park roads. Amenities include a playground area; summertime 40-by-110-foot swimming pool and 10-by-30-foot wading pool; sand volleyball and horseshoes pits; a basketball goal; and a large open area for baseball, soccer, football, and kite flying.

1.8   Fort Griffin State Park and Historic Site

Location: Albany
Entrance fee: Small fee
Season: Open year-round
Camping sites: 20 sites with water and electric hookups; 3 sites with water, electricity, and sewer hookups; 5 tent sites with water only
Maximum length: No length restrictions on sites with full hookups
Facilities: Restroom with showers; dump station; picnic sites, including a group area; enclosed winterized shelter (can be heated in winter and opened in summer) with tables, a grill, electricity, water, and restrooms nearby; two group equestrian camps with water for horses only (combined capacity of 35 rigs)
Fees per night: $$-$$$
Management: Texas Parks & Wildlife Department
Contact: (325) 762-3592
Finding the campground: To reach the park, travel 15 miles north of Albany on US 283. Turn on Park Road 54, which will take you to the campground.
About the campground: The park offers hiking, fishing, picnicking, living history, historical reen-actments, and nature study, with its interpretive center, amphitheater, 3 miles of historic hiking trails, and 1.5 miles of nature trails. Playgrounds with slides and swings, a Texas State Park Store, basketball and volleyball courts, horseshoes pits, and a baseball field are also available. A por-tion of the official Texas longhorn herd resides in the park. The partially restored ruins of Old Fort Griffin—including a hand-dug well, mess hall, barracks, library, rock chimney, store, administration building, cistern, hospital, powder magazine, foundation of the officers' quarters, and first ser-geant's quarters—along with a restored bakery and replicas of enlisted men's huts are on a bluff overlooking the town site of Fort Griffin and the Clear Fork of the Brazos River Valley.

1.9   Fort Richardson State Park and Historic Site, and Lost Creek Reservoir State Trailway

Location: Jacksboro
Entrance fee: Small fee
Season: Open year-round
Camping sites: 37 sites with electric and water hookups; 5 sites with sewer, electric, and water hookups; 20 hike-in (0.5 mile minimum) primitive sites; 11 screened sites, 3 with water and electricity hookups, 8 with full hookups
Fees per night: $-$$
Maximum length: No length restrictions
Facilities: Restrooms with and without showers, dump station, screened shelters
Management: Texas Parks & Wildlife Department
Contact: (940) 567-3506

Finding the campground: To reach the park, travel 0.5 mile south of Jacksboro on TX 199.

About the campground: The fort site includes seven of the original buildings, all of which have been restored: the post hospital, the commanding officer's quarters, a powder magazine, a morgue, a commissary, a guardhouse, and a bakery, which once baked 600 loaves a day. There are also two replica officers' and enlisted men's barracks. The officers' barrack houses the interpretive center. The park's activities and amenities include picnicking, fishing, hiking, biking, horseback riding, nature study, wading in the creek (seasonal), swimming (accessible via Lost Creek Reservoir State Trailway or by road), a volleyball court, horseshoes pits, and a Texas State Park Store.

Lost Creek Reservoir State Trailway, a hike, bike, and equestrian trail, runs adjacent to Fort Richardson. The approximately 10-mile-long trail follows scenic Lost Creek and travels the east side of Lake Jacksboro and Lost Creek Reservoir. Most of the trail travels by the creek or lakes, which provide numerous opportunities to fish and swim. The Prickly Pear Trail takes you through open prairie land for 2 miles, and a nature walk follows Lost Creek for 0.25 mile. Fishing is allowed in the 8-acre Quarry Lake, located by park headquarters.

1.10   Lake Arrowhead State Park

Location: Wichita Falls
Entrance fee: Small fee
Season: Open year-round
Camping sites: 48 sites with 50-amp electric and water hookups; 19 sites with water hookups; 4 equestrian sites with 50-amp electric and water hookups; 5 walk-in primitive group areas
Maximum length: No length restrictions
Facilities: Restrooms with and without showers, dump station; equestrian sites have a picnic table, fire ring, tie rail, corral, and 4 covered stalls
Fees per night: $–$$$
Management: Texas Parks & Wildlife Department
Contact: (940) 528-2211
Finding the campground: From Wichita Falls, travel south on TX 281 for approximately 7 miles, then turn left on FM 1954 for 7 miles. The park is 14 miles from Wichita Falls.
About the campground: Lake Arrowhead State Park is a participant in the "Loan A Tackle Program," which loans fishing tackle. The park features picnic sites with shade; an 18-hole disc golf course; 5 miles of trails; a concrete boat-launching ramp; lighted fishing piers; two fish-cleaning shelters, one at the boat ramp and one at the fishing pier; a floating boat dock; and a 300-acre day-use equestrian area.

1.11   Lake Brownwood State Park

Location: Lake Brownwood
Entrance fee: Small fee
Season: Open year-round
Camping sites: 11 sites with 20/30-amp electric and water hookups in Comanche Trails area; 35 sites with 30/50-amp electric and water hookups in Willow Point; 20 sites with 20/30/50-amp electric, water, and sewer hookups in Council Bluff; 9 tent-only sites with electric and water; 12 tent-only sites with water
Maximum length: No length restrictions
Facilities: Restrooms with and without showers, dump station; picnic table and grill at each site. All campsites have picnic tables.
Fees per night: $$–$$$
Management: Texas Parks & Wildlife Department
Contact: (325) 784-5223
Finding the campground: From Brownwood, take TX 279 northwest for 16 miles and exit on Park Road 15. Travel east on Park Road 15 for 6 miles to reach the park.
About the campground: Activities including picnicking, hiking on 3 miles of trails (including a 0.5-mile nature trail), boating, waterskiing, fishing, swimming, nature study, and bird-watching. The park offers a fish-cleaning facility, a fishing pier with lights, boat-launching ramps, and a floating boat dock with boat slips.

1.12   Lake Colorado City State Park

Location: Colorado City
Entrance fee: Small fee
Season: Open year-round
Camping sites: 69 sites with electric and water hookups; 34 sites with water; 9 premium pull-through sites with electric and water
Maximum length: No length restrictions on sites with full hookups
Facilities: Restrooms with showers, dump station, picnic tables with grills, drinking water
Fees per night: $$–$$$
Management: Texas Parks & Wildlife Department
Contact: (325) 728-3931
Finding the campground: The park is located off I-20 about 6 miles south of Colorado City on FM 2836. Exit on I-20, exit 210.
About the campground: Activities include picnicking, fishing, hiking, and swimming. Containing more than 5 miles of shoreline, the 500-acre park affords numerous outdoor activities for lake swimmers, anglers, water and jet skiers, and naturalists, with its lighted fishing pier, four-lane concrete boat ramp, and 1-mile hiking/nature trail. The park also has a Texas State Park Store.

1.13   Palo Duro Canyon State Park

Location: 12 miles east of Canyon
Entrance fee: Small fee
Season: Open year-round
Camping sites: 79 sites with water and 30- or 50-amp electric hookups; 25 primitive backpack sites (0.5 to 2 miles in); 10 primitive equestrian sites
Maximum length: 50 feet
Facilities: Hookup sites have restrooms with showers nearby and a dump station. Backpack sites have potable water at trailhead and restrooms 0.25 mile from parking area; pets allowed overnight. Equestrian sites have water, and some have pens for horses (4 with and 6 without). Backpack primitive area is 0.5 to 0.75 mile in; no ground fires, containerized fuel only, water 0.5 to 0.75 mile away.
Fees per night: $$–$$$
Management: Texas Parks & Wildlife Department
Contact: (806) 488-2227
Finding the campground: The park is located about 12 miles east of Canyon on TX 217. From Amarillo, take I-27 south to TX 217, and go east 8 miles. From Amarillo, take I-27 south for 18 miles to Canyon, then travel east on TX 217 to the park.
About the campground: Welcome to the Grand Canyon of Texas—Palo Duro Canyon State Park. Activities here include horseback riding, hiking, nature study, bird-watching, mountain biking, and scenic driving.

1.14   Possum Kingdom State Park

Location: Caddo, located near Graham and Mineral Wells
Entrance fee: Small fee
Season: Open year-round
Camping sites: 40 sites with electric and water hookups; 21 premium sites with electric and water; 55 sites with water only; 20 walk-in primitive sites
Maximum length: No length restrictions on sites with full hookups
Facilities: Restrooms with showers, dump station, picnic tables
Fees per night: $–$$$
Management: Texas Parks & Wildlife Department
Contact: (940) 549-1803
Finding the campground: Take US 180 west to Caddo from Dallas about 100 miles, then go 17 miles north on Park Road 33.

About the campground: Activities include picnicking, hiking, biking, nature study, lake swimming, fishing, boating, and waterskiing. A fishing pier, fish-cleaning facility, and concrete boat ramp with a courtesy dock are available, along with playgrounds and 2 miles of hiking/nature trails. The park has a privately operated marina and store, which carries groceries, bait and tackle, miscellaneous camping supplies, firewood, and a large assortment of T-shirts and souvenirs. The marina offers both motorized and nonmotorized boat rentals, covered slip rentals, and a gas dock. Reservations are strongly recommended for motorized boat and slip rentals; call (940) 549-5612.

1.15 San Angelo State Park

Location: San Angelo
Entrance fee: Small fee
Season: Open year-round
Camping sites: 103 developed drive-up sites; 60 sites with electric and water hookups in Red Arroyo section; 11 sites with electric and water hookups in Bald Eagle Creek section (horses are allowed; pens and tethers not provided, but equestrians may bring portable pens); 10 equestrian sites with electric and water hookups in North Concho section (pens furnished); 93 backpack primitive sites in Grandview and River Bend sections, accessible by foot, horseback, or bike (distances range from 5 to 20 miles)
Maximum length: No length restrictions on sites with full hookups
Facilities: Restrooms with showers, dump station. Developed drive-up sites have a picnic table and grill; most sites are covered. Most primitive backpack areas have water spigots and pit toilets; everything packed in must be packed out.
Fees per night: $-$$
Management: Texas Parks & Wildlife Department
Contact: (325) 949-8935
Finding the campground: To reach the park from San Angelo, take US 67 south 2.5 miles to FM 2288 to the south shore entrance, or take US 87 north 0.5 mile to FM 2288 south to the north shore entrance.
About the campground: Activities include picnicking, a three-level orienteering course, and bird and wildlife observation. The lake offers swimming, fishing, and boating, with a fishing platform and dock and high-level and low-level boat ramps. Hiking, mountain biking, and horseback riding can be enjoyed on 50 miles of developed multiuse trails, and there are an additional 20 miles of backpacking trails. The park has a hunting program for hunters with a State Park Annual Hunting Permit and special-drawing hunts for deer and spring turkey. Regularly scheduled tours are given of the ancient Permian animal tracks and Indian petroglyphs. Contact the park for a tour schedule and fees.

Lake Meredith National Recreation Area

	Campsites	Total Sites	Max RV Length	Hookups	Toilets	Showers	Drinking Water	Dump Station	Recreation	Fee
1.16 Blue Creek Bridge	T	*	N/A		NF				HFR	**
1.17 Blue West	T	*	N/A		NF				HFBL	**
1.18 Bugbee	T	*	N/A		NF				HFBL	**
1.19 Cedar Canyon	T	*	N/A		F		X	X	HFLB	**
1.20 Fritch Fortress	TR	*	40		F		X	X	HFLB	**
1.21 Harbor Bay	T	*	N/A		NF			X	HFLB	**
1.22 McBride Canyon	T	*	N/A		NF				H	**
1.23 Mullinaw	T	*	N/A		NF				HR	**
1.24 Plum Creek	T	*	N/A		NF				HRC	**
1.25 Rosita	T	*	N/A		NF				HRC	**
1.26 Sanford-Yake	TR	*	40		F		X	X	HFLB	**

* The National Park Service does not list number of campsites on individual campgrounds.
** No fee

Contrasting spectacularly with its surroundings, Lake Meredith lies on the dry and windswept high plains of the Texas Panhandle. Eleven different campgrounds offer a wide range of camping opportunities, whether you like designated campgrounds with tables, awnings, and grills, or backcountry areas that are more primitive. Campers may stay up to fourteen days.

Dramatic 200-foot canyons carved by the Canadian River surround this 10,000-acre reservoir. The lake was created to supply water for eleven Panhandle cities and to create recreational opportunities such as fishing, boating, waterskiing, sailing, sailboarding, scuba diving, and swimming. Boating is a popular family activity at Lake Meredith. The backcountry surrounding the lake provides areas for hunting, camping, horseback riding, wildlife viewing, and hiking.

Anglers can enjoy fishing for several different species, including walleye, crappie, bass, catfish, and trout. Lake Meredith hosts several fishing tournaments each year. One of the most popular is the Small Fry Fishing Tournament, held in cooperation with the Texas Parks & Wildlife Department, which promotes the sport of fishing for children.

Game species found at Lake Meredith include white-tailed and mule deer, dove, turkey, quail, duck, pheasant, and goose. Hunting is allowed during game-specific sea-

sons. All hunters are required to have a Texas State Hunting License. A Federal Duck
Stamp is also required for those hunting migratory waterfowl.

1.16 Lake Meredith National Recreation Area–Blue Creek Bridge

Location: Fritch
Entrance fee: None
Season: Open year-round
Camping sites: No designated sites
Maximum length: There are no hookups for RVs but there are lots of camping areas for the vehicles. The park is never full.
Facilities: Chemical toilets, picnic tables; no water
Fees per night: None
Management: National Park Service
Contact: (806) 857-3151
Finding the campground: From Amarillo, take TX 136 north 40 miles to Fritch. Headquarters are located at 419 E. Broadway in Fritch. If coming from the north on US 87/287, take FM 1913 east for 15.6 miles.
About the campground: This area is one of two designated off-road-vehicle use areas. Off-road vehicles, however, are restricted to the creek bed.

1.17 Lake Meredith National Recreation Area–Blue West

Location: North side of Lake Meredith
Entrance fee: None
Camping sites: Beachfront camping; no developed sites
Maximum length: Generally not suitable for RVs
Facilities: Picnic tables, shade shelters, and some grills at sites; vault toilets; no drinking water
Fees per night: None
Management: National Park Service
Contact: (806) 857-3151
Finding the campground: From Amarillo, take TX 136 north 40 miles to Fritch. Headquarters are located at 419 E. Broadway in Fritch. If coming from the north on US 87/287, take FM 1913 east for 15.6 miles.
About the campground: There is an excellent view of the lake from this campground, but access to the water from the campground's shoreline is difficult. However, a public boat ramp is located nearby (small launch fee). Blue West is seldom full.

1.18 Lake Meredith National Recreation Area–
Bugbee

Location: Fritch
Entrance fee: None
Season: Open year-round
Camping sites: Semi-developed camping area with no individual sites (availability changes with fluctuating lake levels)
Maximum length: Generally not suitable for RVs
Facilities: Chemical toilets, picnic tables; no water
Fees per night: None
Management: National Park Service
Contact: (806) 857-3151
Finding the campground: From Amarillo, take exit TX 136 north 40 miles to Fritch. Headquarters are located at 419 E. Broadway in Fritch. If coming from the north on US 87/287, take FM 1913 east for 15.6 miles.
About the campground: Bugbee campground is popular with shoreline anglers. A public boat ramp is located nearby (small launch fee).

1.19 Lake Meredith National Recreation Area–
Cedar Canyon

Location: Fritch
Entrance fee: None
Season: Open year-round
Camping sites: No designated sites (availability changes with fluctuating lake levels)
Maximum length: Generally not suitable for RVs
Facilities: Restroom (open seasonally) with running water and flush toilets in the boat ramp parking lot; dump station at head of the Cedar Canyon entrance road
Fees per night: None
Management: National Park Service
Contact: (806) 857-3151
Finding the campground: From Amarillo, take TX 136 north 40 miles to Fritch. Headquarters are located at 419 E. Broadway in Fritch. If coming from the north on US 87/287, take FM 1913 east for 15.6 miles.
About the campground: Cedar Canyon, located on the shore of Lake Meredith, is fairly small. A public boat ramp is located nearby (small launch fee).

1.20 Lake Meredith National Recreation Area– Fritch Fortress

Location: Fritch
Entrance fee: None
Season: Open year-round
Camping sites: No designated sites
Maximum length: Pull-through campsites are available, but not suitable for anything over 40 feet
Facilities: Restroom (open seasonally) with running water and flush toilets; dump station nearby
Fees per night: None
Management: National Park Service
Contact: (806) 857-3151
Finding the campground: From Amarillo, take TX 136 north 40 miles to Fritch. Headquarters are located at 419 E. Broadway in Fritch. If coming from the north on US 87/287, take FM 1913 east for 15.6 miles.
About the campground: Beautiful views from this bluff location make Fritch Fortress an attractive campground. A public boat ramp is nearby (small launch fee).

1.21 Lake Meredith National Recreation Area– Harbor Bay

Location: Fritch
Entrance fee: None
Season: Open year-round
Camping sites: No individual sites (availability changes with fluctuating lake levels)
Maximum length: Not suitable for RVs
Facilities: Chemical toilets near the public boat ramp, picnic tables, dump station nearby; no drinking water
Fees per night: None
Management: National Park Service
Contact: (806) 857-3151
Finding the campground: From Amarillo, take TX 136 north 40 miles to Fritch. Headquarters are located at 419 E. Broadway in Fritch. If coming from the north on US 87/287, take FM 1913 east for 15.6 miles.
About the campground: Harbor Bay, a shoreline campground located just outside the community of Fritch, becomes extremely crowded on summer holiday weekends. The access road is blacktop, but the camping area can become soft during rainy conditions. A public boat ramp is nearby (small launch fee).

1.22 Lake Meredith National Recreation Area– McBride Canyon

Location: Fritch
Entrance fee: None
Season: Open year-round
Camping sites: No designated sites
Maximum length: Not suitable for RVs
Facilities: Chemical toilets, picnic tables; no water
Fees per night: None
Management: National Park Service
Contact: (806) 857-3151
Finding the campground: From Amarillo, take TX 136 north 40 miles to Fritch. Headquarters are located at 419 E. Broadway in Fritch. If coming from the north on US 87/287, take FM 1913 east for 15.6 miles.
About the campground: McBride Canyon campground is a beautiful area with huge cottonwood trees shading the picnic areas. Note that the dirt access road can become impassable during and after rain. No access to the lake from this campground.

1.23 Lake Meredith National Recreation Area– Mullinaw

Location: Fritch
Entrance fee: None
Season: Open year-round
Camping sites: Undeveloped sites
Maximum length: Not suitable for RVs
Facilities: Chemical toilets, picnic tables; no water
Fees per night: None
Management: National Park Service
Contact: (806) 857-3151
Finding the campground: From Amarillo, take TX 136 north 40 miles to Fritch. Headquarters are located at 419 E. Broadway in Fritch. If coming from the north on US 87/287, take FM 1913 east for 15.6 miles.
About the campground: Horseback riding is allowed.

1.24 Lake Meredith National Recreation Area– Plum Creek

Location: Fritch
Entrance fee: None
Season: Open year-round
Camping sites: No designated sites
Maximum length: Generally not suitable for RVs
Facilities: Chemical toilets, picnic tables; no water
Fees per night: None
Management: National Park Service
Contact: (806) 857-3151
Finding the campground: From Amarillo, take TX 136 north 40 miles to Fritch. Headquarters are located at 419 E. Broadway in Fritch. If coming from the north on US 87/287, take FM 1913 east for 15.6 miles.
About the campground: This area contains some large shade trees and is quite popular with hunters and horseback riders. Hitch rails and horse pens are provided. Devil's Canyon Trail is used by equestrians, hikers, and mountain bikers.

1.25 Lake Meredith National Recreation Area– Rosita

Location: Fritch, along the Canadian River
Entrance fee: None
Season: Open year-round
Camping sites: No designated sites
Maximum length: Generally not suitable for RVs
Facilities: Chemical toilets, picnic tables; no water
Fees per night: None
Management: National Park Service
Contact: (806) 857-3151
Finding the campground: From Amarillo, take TX 136 north 40 miles to Fritch. Headquarters are located at 419 E. Broadway in Fritch. If coming from the north on US 87/287, take FM 1913 east for 15.6 miles.
About the campground: Rosita is one of two off-road-vehicle use areas and is also a horseback-riding area.

1.26 Lake Meredith National Recreation Area– Sanford-Yake

Location: Fritch

Entrance fee: None

Season: Open year-round

Camping sites: Basic campsites located close to marina

Maximum length: 40 feet

Facilities: Picnic area, shade shelter, and grill at each site; central comfort station with running water and flush toilets (open seasonally); dump station nearby

Fees per night: None

Management: National Park Service

Contact: (806) 857-3151

Finding the campground: From Amarillo, take TX 136 north 40 miles to Fritch. Headquarters are located at 419 E. Broadway in Fritch. If coming from the north on US 87/287, take FM 1913 east for 15.6 miles.

About the campground: This campground is located on a spectacular bluff overlooking Lake Meredith near the marina, on the Sanford-Yake Road, and is similar to the more traditional National Park Service campgrounds. A public boat ramp is located at the marina (small launch fee).

Prairies and Lakes

The old saying "Everything's bigger in Texas" is especially true when talking about the Prairies and Lakes region. It's the largest of all the travel regions in the Lone Star State, with big cities—Dallas and Fort Worth to name a couple—big attractions, and lots of campgrounds. There are more camping opportunities in the Prairies and Lakes than in any of the other six travel regions, ranging from large campgrounds with all the amenities to small, remote backpack camping experiences. Just about all the campgrounds are located on reservoirs, offering myriad recreational opportunities such as swimming, fishing, and boating, along with hiking, mountain biking, and horseback riding.

The Red River, which separates Texas from Oklahoma, makes up the Prairies and Lakes region's northern border. The region's southern edge is more than 350 miles away, just a little southeast of San Antonio.

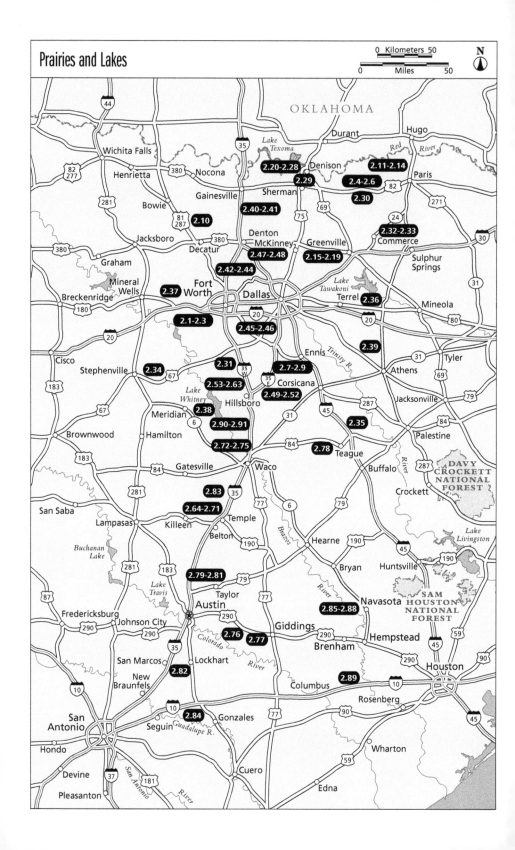

Prairies and Lakes

0 Kilometers 50

0 Miles 50

N

OKLAHOMA

Durant
Hugo

Lake Texoma

44

35

Wichita Falls

82
277

Henrietta

380

Nocona

Red River

2.20-2.28

Denison

2.11-2.14

Paris

Sherman

2.29

2.4-2.6

82

281

Bowie

Gainesville

2.30

271

81
287

2.10

Jacksboro

380

Decatur

Denton
McKinney

69

75

24

2.32-2.33

Commerce

30

380

Graham

2.47-2.48

Greenville

2.15-2.19

Sulphur
Springs

Mineral
Wells

2.42-2.44

Fort

2.37

31

Breckenridge

180

Worth

Dallas

Lake
Tawakoni

Terrel

2.36

Mineola

80

2.1-2.3

20

20

20

2.45-2.46

Ennis

Trinity R.

2.39

31

Tyler

Cisco

Stephenville

2.34

67

2.31

35

35
E

2.7-2.9

Corsicana

Athens

69

183

Lake
Whitney

2.53-2.63

2.49-2.52

287

Jacksonville

79

Meridian

2.38

Hillsboro

31

45

2.35

84

Palestine

Brownwood

Hamilton

6

2.90-2.91

183

2.72-2.75

84

2.78

Teague

Buffalo

River

DAVY
CROCKETT
NATIONAL
FOREST

84

Gatesville

Waco

79

Crockett

281

2.83

35

San Saba

2.64-2.71

77

6

79

Lake
Livingston

Lampasas

Killeen

Temple

Buchanan
Lake

281

183

Belton

190

Hearne

190

45

190

Bryan

Huntsville

SAM
HOUSTON
NATIONAL
FOREST

87

Fredericksburg

Johnson City

290

290

2.79-2.81

79

Taylor

77

Lake
Travis

Austin

290

Navasota

Hempstead

59

290

San Marcos

35

2.76

2.77

Giddings

290

Brenham

290

45

Colorado River

Lockhart

River

Houston

New
Braunfels

2.82

Columbus

2.89

10

Rosenberg

90

45

10

San
Antonio

10

2.84

Seguin

Gonzales

77

90

Guadalupe R.

Hondo

Wharton

59

Devine

37

181

Cuero

Edna

Pleasanton

San Antonio River

Benbrook Lake and Caddo National Grasslands

	Campsites	Total Sites	Max RV Length	Hookups	Toilets	Showers	Drinking Water	Dump Station	Recreation	Fee
2.1 Benbrook Lake—Holiday Park RA	TRS	105	U	WE	F	X	X	X	HSFBLRC	$$–$$$
2.2 Benbrook Lake—Mustang RA	TR	40	U	WES	F	X	X	X	HSFBLRC	$$$
2.3 Benbrook Lake—Rocky Creek RA	TR	11	U		F		X	X	SFBL	$$
2.4 Caddo Nat'l Grasslands— Coffee Mill Lake RA	TR	15	U	W	NF		X		FBL	$
2.5 Caddo Nat'l Grasslands— East Lake Crockett RA	T	7	U	W	NF		X		FBL	$
2.6 Caddo Nat'l Grasslands— West Lake Crockett RA	TR	12	25	W	NF		X		HF	$

Benbrook Lake is located in rolling hills and prairie meadows close to the major metropolitan area of Fort Worth. Picnicking, fishing, hunting, boating, bird-watching, hiking, and horseback riding are just a few of the activities available to Benbrook Lake campers.

The Caddo National Grasslands are located northeast of the Dallas/Fort Worth metroplex. In addition to providing grazing land for cattle and habitat for wildlife, the grasslands offer a variety of recreation. The most popular activities are hiking, camping, fishing, hunting, horseback riding, mountain biking, wildlife viewing, and photography.

White-tailed deer, coyotes, bobcats, red foxes and other small mammals, water-fowl, bobwhite quail, turkey, and songbirds thrive in the diverse habitats provided by the Caddo Grasslands. Largemouth bass, blue and channel catfish, and various sunfish species are common catches at the many lakes that dot the grasslands' landscape.

2.1 Benbrook Lake–Holiday Park Recreation Area

Location: Benbrook
Entrance fee: None
Season: Open year-round
Camping sites: 65 sites with 20/30-amp electric and water hookups, 5 of which have enclosed screened shelters; 6 sites with 50-amp electric and water hookups; 34 sites with no hookups
Maximum length: No length restrictions
Facilities: Covered table, parking space, and cooker at each site; dump station; restrooms with flush toilets and showers; drinking-water hydrants and fountains scattered throughout park
Fees per night: $$–$$$
Management: U.S. Army Corps of Engineers
Contact: (817) 292-2400
Finding the campground: From I-20, take exit 429A to US 377 and go 4.5 miles southwest to the lake.
About the campground: Holiday Park is the largest campground on Benbrook Lake, with 105 designated campsites. Many of these campsites may be reserved through the National Recreation Reservation Service (NRRS). Holiday Park has several miles of shoreline with a generally gentle slope, making it popular for swimming, while the 1.5-mile-long dam top is enjoyed by joggers and bicyclists. Bird-watching, hiking, and fishing are other popular activities at Benbrook Lake. Hunting in season is also allowed with a permit from the Army Corps of Engineers office.

Benbrook Lake provides many excellent fishing opportunities. Texas Parks & Wildlife stocks the lake every few years, and Benbrook was one of the first Texas lakes to be stocked with Florida-strain largemouth bass in the early 1980s. The lake record for largemouth bass is over 13 pounds. White bass, hybrid white/striped bass, crappie, channel and flathead catfish, sunfish, carp, and buffalo are abundant in the lake. Spring runs of white bass and hybrids up the river and creek channels provide an especially good chance to take fish from the shoreline.

Both the Benbrook and Rocky Creek marinas provide enclosed fishing barges. Boat ramps at either end of the park have courtesy docks for assistance with loading and unloading of campers' boats. A fishing pier is located at the park's south end. There is no boat launch fee if you are camping in the park.

2.2 Benbrook Lake–Mustang Park and Mustang Point Recreation Areas

Location: Benbrook
Entrance fee: None
Season: Open year-round

Camping sites: 34 sites with 20/30-amp electric and water hookups; 6 sites with 50-amp electric and water hookups, 2 of which also have sewer hookups. No designated primitive campsites, but campers are free to pull into any spot near the shoreline and set up their tent or RV.

Maximum length: No length restrictions

Facilities: Covered table, parking space, and cooker at each site; dump station; 3 restrooms, 1 with showers; group camping facility consisting of a large pavilion with parking, lights, water and electric outlets, and 6 individual campsites, each with its own parking, hookups, and individual covered table

Fees per night: $$$

Management: U.S. Army Corps of Engineers

Contact: (817) 292-2400

Finding the campground: From I-20, take exit 429A to US 377 and go 2.5 miles southwest to the lake, and then Hwy 1187 for 2 miles.

About the campground: Mustang Park, on the south end of Benbrook Lake, is divided into the Bear Creek Campground, with camping facilities comparable to those in Holiday Park, and the Mustang Point Recreation Area Campground. There are two reservable group areas for both day use and overnight camping, along with a designated swim beach and boat-launching ramps. The boat ramps are located at either end of the park for access to both the lake and the channel of Bear Creek. There is a small boat-launching fee, which is included in the camping fee.

2.3   Benbrook Lake–Rocky Creek Recreation Area

Location: Benbrook

Entrance fee: None

Season: Open year-round

Camping sites: 11 basic sites

Maximum length: No length restrictions

Facilities: Restroom on the peninsula and 2 more at other park locations, dump station, drinking-water hydrants and fountains scattered throughout park

Fees per night: $$

Management: U.S. Army Corps of Engineers

Contact: (817) 292-2400

Finding the campground: From I-20, take exit 429A to US 377 and go 2.5 miles southwest to the lake, then take Hwy 1187 to Grandbury Road for about to 2 miles to campground.

About the campground: Rocky Creek Park, on the east side of the lake, provides day-use and picnic areas. Rocky Creek Campground has primitive campsites under tree cover along the Rocky and Primrose Branch creek channels. The campground provides access to an open peninsula with lots of shoreline for picnicking, swimming, and fishing. Picnicking is allowed anywhere on the peninsula area, not only at the several covered table sites. The Rocky Creek Marina (817-346-2199) also offers campsites, along with other facilities and activities. There is a small boat-launching fee, which is included in the camping fee.

2.4 Caddo National Grasslands– Coffee Mill Lake Recreation Area

Location: Honey Grove
Entrance fee: Day-use fee
Season: Open year-round
Camping sites: 15 basic sites (tents and limited RV space)
Maximum length: No size restriction
Facilities: Pit toilets, drinking water
Fees per night: Overnight camping included in day-use fee ($)
Management: USDA Forest Service
Contact: (940) 627-5475
Finding the campground: From Honey Grove, follow FM 100 north 12 miles to FM 409. Turn left and go west 5 miles to the campground entrance on the left.
About the campground: Coffee Mill Lake (651 acres) has a developed recreation area containing 13 picnic units and an improved boat ramp. The lake offers boating and fishing. The paved boat ramp is accessible from a loop road around the camping area. Hybrid bass, catfish, crappie, and bluegill are stocked regularly.

2.5 Caddo National Grasslands– East Lake Crockett Recreation Area

Location: Honey Grove
Entrance fee: Day-use fee
Season: Open year-round
Camping sites: Limited camping
Maximum length: N/A
Facilities: Pit toilets, drinking water
Fees per night: Overnight camping included in day-use fee ($)
Management: USDA Forest Service
Contact: (940) 627-5475
Finding the campground: From Honey Grove, follow FM 100 north 12 miles to FM 409. Turn left and go west 5 miles to the campground entrance on the left.
About the campground: East Lake Crockett Recreation Area is located on the northeast shore of the 450-acre Lake Crockett. The lake is stocked with catfish, sunfish, crappie, and bass. A paved boat ramp and fishing pier are accessible from the parking lot.

2.6 Caddo National Grasslands–West Lake Crockett Recreation Area

Location: Honey Grove
Entrance fee: Day-use fee
Season: Open year-round
Camping sites: 12 RV and tent sites
Maximum length: 25 feet
Facilities: Pit toilets, drinking water
Fees per night: Overnight camping included in day-use fee ($)
Management: USDA Forest Service
Contact: (940) 627-5475
Finding the campground: From Honey Grove, follow FM 100 north 12 miles to FM 409. Turn left and go west 2 miles to camp entrance on the left.
About the campground: West Lake Crockett Recreation Area is located on the northwest shore of the 450-acre Lake Crockett, which offers fishing from the shore. Hiking trails are accessible from this campground.

Lake Bardwell and Lyndon B. Johnson National Grasslands

	Campsites	Total Sites	Max RV Length	Hookups	Toilets	Showers	Drinking Water	Dump Station	Recreation	Fee
2.7 Lake Bardwell–Highview RA	TR	39	40	EW	F, NF	X	X	X	SFBLR	$$
2.8 Lake Bardwell–Mott RA	TR	40	40	EW	F, NF	X	X	X	SFBLR	$$
2.9 Lake Bardwell–Waxahachie Creek RA	TR	76	40	EW	F, NF	X	X	X	SFBLR	$$
2.10 Lyndon B. Johnson Nat'l Grasslands–Black Creek Lake	T	7	N/A	N/A	NF				HFBL	$

Lake Bardwell, located close to Ennis, offers a wide variety of outdoor recreation opportunities for the camper, including fishing, boating, hiking, and swimming. The newest recreational activity is horseback riding. The Bardwell Lake equestrian and multiuse trail is on a 2,000-acre tract of land at the north end of Waxahachie Creek.

Currently there are over 13 miles of trails for horseback riding, bicycling, or hiking, providing a possible round-trip of 26 miles. The trailhead is located near the northernmost boat ramp at Waxahachie Creek Park. The system features one broad, flat main trail traversing the area, with numerous loops into the surrounding upland wooded thickets, meadows, croplands, and bottomland hardwood forest along the creek. These trails are designated with color-coded signs and international symbols.

For the angler, 3,138-acre Lake Bardwell offers good to excellent fishing opportunities for white and hybrid striped bass and crappie.

Local anglers consider Bardwell Lake one of the best-kept secrets in the state. Although the largemouth bass caught from Bardwell may not be in the trophy category, bass anglers usually get their lines stretched. Crappie fishing is best at either Highview Marina, under the TX 34 bridge, or in Waxahachie and Mustang Creeks during spawning. Fishing for catfish is usually excellent, especially when the lake elevation is gradually rising.

Bardwell Lake has boat ramps at five parks: Love, Mott, Highview, Waxahachie, and Little Mustang Creek. These ramps are of concrete construction with four lanes. Favorite spots to try your luck if you don't have a boat are the fishing piers at the marina. Two of the piers are enclosed for the convenience of customers during inclement weather. A small fee is charged for the use of these facilities.

Black Creek Lake Campground offers only tent camping, but remote fishing and hiking activities are available within a short distance. Cottonwood Lake, approximately 40 acres in size, is located 5 miles north of Black Creek Lake and has an improved boat ramp. The Cottonwood–Black Creek Trail is 4 miles long and connects the two lakes. There are nearly 75 miles of multipurpose trails that run in the Cottonwood Lake–Black Creek vicinity.

Lyndon B. Johnson National Grasslands is known for its great hiking trails. There are lots of different trail types—climbing or flat, woods, and open fields. The Grasslands is a long way away from civilization allowing hikers to be close to nature.

2.7 Lake Bardwell–Highview Recreation Area

Location: 3 miles southwest of Ennis
Entrance fee: None
Season: Open year-round
Camping sites: 39 sites with 30- or 50-amp electric and water hookups
Maximum length: 40 feet
Facilities: Restroom with flush toilets and showers, 2 vault toilets, dump station
Fees per night: $$
Management: U.S. Army Corps of Engineers
Contact: (972) 875-5711
Finding the campground: From Dallas, head south on I-45 for 36.4 miles to exit 247, US 287 North/Congressman Joe Barton Parkway, toward Waxahachie/Fort Worth. Travel north 3.4 miles to Ensign Road, then turn left and go 1.5 miles to the Bardwell Lake Headquarters office.
About the campground: Highview Recreation Area is located on the west side of the lake and consists of approximately 155 acres, with development on 84 acres. A paved county road leading from TX 34 provides access to the park. Camping, fishing, and picnicking are just a few of the recreational opportunities at Bardwell Lake, which also offers a four-lane boat ramp (small launch fee), two courtesy docks, a full-service marina, and a designated swimming beach (small day-use fee).

2.8 Lake Bardwell–Mott Recreation Area

Location: 3 miles southwest of Ennis
Entrance fee: None
Season: Open Apr through Sept
Camping sites: 33 sites with water and electric hookups; 7 sites without hookups
Maximum length: 40 feet

Facilities: Restroom with flush toilets and showers, vault toilet, dump station
Fees per night: $$
Management: U.S. Army Corps of Engineers
Contact: (972) 875-5711
Finding the campground: From Dallas, head south on I-45 for 36.4 miles to exit 247, US 287 North/Congressman Joe Barton Parkway, toward Waxahachie/Fort Worth. Travel north 3.4 miles to Ensign Road, then turn left and go 1.5 miles to the Bardwell Lake Headquarters office.
About the campground: Mott Recreation Area consists of approximately 270 acres, with development on approximately 54 acres, and is located on the west side of the lake. A four-lane boat ramp (small launching fee), a courtesy dock, two designated fishing areas, and a swimming beach (small day-use fee) are available.

2.9   Lake Bardwell–Waxahachie Creek Recreation Area

Location: 3 miles southwest of Ennis
Entrance fee: None
Season: Open year-round
Camping sites: 69 sites with water and electric hookups; 7 sites without hookups
Maximum length: 40 feet
Facilities: Pull-through campsites, dump station, 4 vault toilets, 2 shower facilities
Fees per night: $$
Management: U.S. Army Corps of Engineers
Contact: (972) 875-5711
Finding the campground: From Dallas, head south on I-45 for 36.4 miles to exit 247, US 287 North/Congressman Joe Barton Parkway, towards Waxahachie/Fort Worth. Go north 3.4 miles to Ensign Road, then turn left and go 1.5 miles to the Bardwell Lake Headquarters office.
About the campground: The park is located in the upper reaches of the lake along the Waxahachie Creek arm and consists of approximately 205 acres, with development on 63 acres. One four-lane boat ramp (small launching fee), picnic areas, a swimming beach (small day-use fee), and equestrian and walking trails are available.

2.10 Lyndon B. Johnson National Grasslands– Black Creek Lake

Location: Decatur
Entrance fee: Day-use fee
Season: Open year-round
Camping sites: 7 walk-in sites
Maximum length: N/A
Facilities: Pit toilets; no drinking water
Fees per night: Overnight camping included in day-use fee ($)
Management: USDA Forest Service
Contact: (940) 627-5475
Finding the campground: From Hwy 287 in Decatur go north for 4.5 miles, turn right on CR 2175, cross over the railroad tracks and go an additional 1 mile. At that point, turn left on old Decatur Road, go 4 miles, turn right on CR 2372. You should see a sign for Black Creek Lake. Go 2 miles and turn left on CR 2461 for 0.05 mile. Take the first left on FS 902 to the campground.
About the campground: The LBJ is composed of more than 20,250 acres, with a developed recreation area located at Black Creek Lake, which is approximately 30 acres in size. Cottonwood Lake, located 5 miles north of Black Creek Lake, is about 40 acres and has an improved boat ramp. No recreation facilities are provided. The Cottonwood–Black Creek Trail is 4 miles long and connects the two lakes. It is rated moderately difficult. There are nearly 75 miles of multipurpose trails in the Cottonwood Lake vicinity. Other popular lakes include Clear Lake and Rhodes Lake. Clear Lake is approximately 20 acres in size and has a concrete boat ramp and a 50-foot wheelchair-accessible fishing pier. Rhodes Lake is about 15 acres and has no facilities. Black Creek Lake has seven picnic units.

Pat Mayse Lake

	Campsites	Total Sites	Max RV Length	Hookups	Toilets	Showers	Drinking Water	Dump Station	Recreation	Fee
2.11 Lamar Point RA	TR	27	40	WP	F, NF	X	X	X	SFBL	$$
2.12 East RA	TR	26	40	EW	NF		X		FBL	$$
2.13 West RA	TR	86	40	EWP	F, NF	X	X	X	SFBL	$$
2.14 Sanders Cove RA	TR	89	40	EWP	F, NF	X	X	X	SFBL	$$

Pat Mayse Lake is a favorite among campers who enjoy a developed park. The lake provides excellent opportunities for fishing and hunting. Sport fish species include largemouth bass, striped bass, white crappie, sunfish, and channel and flathead catfish, among others. These lands are managed for upland game and white-tailed deer and are open to the public during hunting seasons. Game species include deer, fox squirrel, gray squirrel, bobwhite quail, morning dove, cottontail rabbit, raccoon, and fox. Fur bearers such as opossum, beaver, mink, skunk, and nutria are also present.

Pay Mayse Lake also provides resting and feeding habitat for migratory waterfowl. A few miles north of the project area are the famed Red River Bottoms, where waterfowl congregate in great numbers.

2.11 Pat Mayse Lake–Lamar Point Recreation Area

Location: 4 miles northwest of Powderly
Entrance fee: None
Season: Open year-round
Camping sites: 27 basic sites
Maximum length: 40 feet
Facilities: Restrooms with flush toilets and showers, vault toilets, drinking water, dump station, telephone, and there is no electricity at Lamar Point
Fees per night: $$
Management: U.S. Army Corps of Engineers
Contact: (903) 732-3020

Finding the campground: From Paris, take US 271 north for about 5 miles, then west FM 1499 for 8 miles. Then go 3 miles north on FM 1500 to Lamar Point.

About the campground: Pat Mayse Lake offers 6,000 acres of surface water for sporting activities, with two boat ramps (small launch fee included in camping fee) and a swimming area. The upper third of the lake, upstream from Lamar Point, is heavily timbered with numerous coves and cuts that provide excellent habitat for largemouth bass, crappie, and catfish. Many of these coves also have margins of submerged and emergent vegetation.

2.12   Pat Mayse Lake–East Recreation Area

Location: 4 miles northwest of Powderly
Entrance fee: None
Season: Open year-round
Camping sites: 26 sites all with water and electricity
Maximum length: 40 feet
Facilities: Vault toilets
Fees per night: $$
Management: U.S. Army Corps of Engineers
Contact: (903) 732-3020
Finding the campground: From Paris, take TX 271 north for 12 miles to FM 906. Continue west about 3 miles on FM 906 across Pat Mayse dam. You will here meet up with FM 197, going approximately west.

About the campground: The lake provides excellent opportunities for fishing and hunting. Sport fish include largemouth bass, white crappie, sunfish, striped bass, and channel and flathead catfish, along with other common species. Two boat launch ramps are available (small launch fee included in the camping fee). These lands are managed for upland game and white-tailed deer and are open to the public for hunting.

2.13   Pat Mayse Lake–West Recreation Area

Location: 4 miles northwest of Powderly
Entrance fee: None
Season: Open year-round
Camping sites: 81 sites with water and electricity; 5 sites with no electricity
Maximum length: 40 feet
Facilities: Pit and flush toilets, showers, drinking water, dump station, telephone
Fees per night: $$
Management: U.S. Army Corps of Engineers
Contact: (903) 732-3020

Finding the campground: From Paris, take TX 271 north for 12 miles to FM 906 and go west 4 miles to FM 197. Travel west on FM 197 for 3 miles to CR 35810, turn left and go 1 mile to CR 35800, then make another left into the park.

About the campground: The lake provides excellent opportunities for fishing and hunting, along with swimming. Sport fish species include largemouth bass, white crappie, sunfish, striped bass, and channel and flathead catfish, among other common species. There are two boat ramps (small launch fee included in the camping fee) and a courtesy dock. These lands are managed for upland game and white-tailed deer and are open to the public for hunting.

2.14   Pat Mayse Lake–Sanders Cove Recreation Area

Location: 4 miles northwest of Powderly
Entrance fee: None
Season: Open year-round
Camping sites: 81 sites with electric and water hookups; 4 sites without hookups
Maximum length: 40 feet
Facilities: Vault and flush toilets, showers, drinking water, dump station, telephone
Fees per night: $$
Management: U.S. Army Corps of Engineers
Contact: (903) 732-3020
Finding the campground: From Paris, take TX 271 north for 12 miles to FM 906, then 0.75 mile west on FM 906 to Sanders Cove.

About the campground: The lake provides excellent opportunities for fishing and hunting, along with swimming. Sport fish include largemouth bass, white crappie, sunfish, striped bass, and channel and flathead catfish, among other common species. There are two boat ramps (small launch fee included in the camping fee) and a courtesy dock. These lands are managed for upland game and white-tailed deer and are open to the public for hunting.

Lavon Lake

	Campsites	Total Sites	Max RV Length	Hookups	Toilets	Showers	Drinking Water	Dump Station	Recreation	Fee
2.15 Clear Lake Park RA	TR	23	50	WE	F, NF	X	X	X	FBL	$$
2.16 Collin Park RA	TR	68	50	WE	F, NF	X	X	X	FBLJ	$$-$$$
2.17 East Fork Park RA	TR	62	50	WE	F, NF	X	X	X	SFBLR	$$
2.18 Lakeland Park RA	T	32	N/A	W	F		X		FBL	$
2.19 Lavonia Park RA	TR	53	50	WE	F. NF		X	X	FBL	$$

Campers who like to do a little fishing should find Lavon Lake to their liking. Blue and channel catfish are caught in good numbers year-round, along with some flatheads. Look for points, grass, brush, or heavily timbered areas, and more than likely catfish will be there. Some of the well-known catfish hot spots include timbered areas around Brockdale Park. Points off Ticky Creek Park and Little Ridge Park are great areas for springtime drift fishing.

2.15   Lavon Lake–Clear Lake Park Recreation Area

Location: Princeton
Entrance fee: None
Season: Open Apr through Sept
Camping sites: 23 sites with water and electric hookups
Maximum length: 50 feet
Facilities: Restrooms, showers, dump station
Fees per night: $$
Management: U.S. Army Corp of Engineers
Contact: (972) 442-3141
Finding the campground: From US 380 in Princeton, take FM 982 south for approximately 8.5 miles and look for signs designating the park entrance. The campground is located on the west shore of the east arm of the lake.
About the campground: Lots of trees provide ample shade at this campground, which is located on a peninsula providing a good view of the lake and shoreline fishing. There are two four-lane boat ramps (small launch fee included in camping fee), with a courtesy dock at the south ramp, and a fishing pier.

2.16   Lavon Lake–Collin Park Recreation Area

Location: Wylie
Entrance fee: Day-use fee
Season: Open year-round
Camping sites: 56 sites with water and electric hookups; 12 tent-only sites with water
Maximum length: 50 feet
Facilities: Restrooms, showers, dump station
Fees per night: $$–$$$
Management: Collin Park Marina & Campground
Contact: (972) 442-5755
Finding the campground: From US 75 in Plano, take Parker Road east to where it ends at FM 1378. Turn right, then take the first left on FM 2514. Go about 1 mile, turn right, and go 1.5 miles. Watch for signs designating the park entrance. The campground is located downlake on the west shore of the Trinity River arm.
About the campground: Three boat ramps and boat rentals are available at the marina.

2.17   Lavon Lake–East Fork Recreation Area

Location: Wylie
Entrance fee: None
Season: Open year-round
Camping sites: 50 sites with electric and water hookups; 12 tent-only sites with water
Maximum length: 50 feet
Facilities: Restrooms, showers, dump station
Fees per night: $$
Management: U.S. Army Corps of Engineers and East Fork Harbor Marina
Contact: (972) 442-3141
Finding the campground: From Wylie, take TX 78 east, then turn north on CR 389. The park entrance is near the intersection of CR 389 and CR 384, and the campground is located down lake west of the dam.
About the campground: East Fork Recreation Area provides close access to the equestrian Trinity Trail. The campground is located on the western side of Lake Lavon. Two four-lane boat ramps with courtesy docks are available; a small launch fee and swimming beach fee is included in the cost of camping.

2.18   Lavon Lake–Lakeland Park Recreation Area

Location: Farmersville
Entrance fee: None
Season: Open Apr through Sept
Camping sites: 32 primitive tent-only sites
Maximum length: N/A
Facilities: Water at campground, restrooms at boat ramp
Fees per night: $
Management: U.S. Army Corps of Engineers
Contact: (972) 442-3141
Finding the campground: From US 380 in Farmersville, take TX 78 south 4 miles and look for the park entrance on west side of road. The campground is located midlake on the east shore.
About the campground: Lakeland is a camping-only park. The lake has a four-lane boat ramp; a small launch fee is included in the camping fee.

2.19 Lavon Lake–Lavonia Park Recreation Area

Location: Lavon
Entrance fee: None
Season: Open year-round
Camping sites: 38 sites with electric and water hookups; 15 tent-only sites with water
Maximum length: 50 feet
Facilities: Restrooms, dump station
Fees per night: $$
Management: U.S. Army Corps of Engineers
Contact: (972) 442-3141
Finding the campground: From TX 78 north of Lavon, turn right on FM 6 about 3 miles. The campground is located downlake on the east shore.
About the campground: Lavonia is the closest park to the dam, and it also has the largest day-use area of any of the Lavon Lake parks, with 51 picnic tables. There are two boat ramps, one inside the park and one just outside (small launch fee included in camping fee); a courtesy dock is provided at the inside ramp.

Lake Texoma

	Campsites	Total Sites	Max RV Length	Hookups	Toilets	Showers	Drinking Water	Dump Station	Recreation	Fee
2.20 **Big Mineral Camp**	TR	100	U	WESI	F		X	X	FBL	$$-$$$
2.21 **Cedar Mills Marina**	TR	38	U	WES	F	X	X	X	SFBLJ	$$-$$$
2.22 **Damsite RA**	TR	31	U	WE	NF	X	X	X	FBL	$$
2.23 **Grandpappy Point Marina**	TR	56	U	WES	F	-	X	X	FBL	$$-$$$
2.24 **Highport Marina and Resort**	TR	15	U	WES	F	X	X		FBLJ	$$$
2.25 **Juniper Point RA**	TR	70	U	WE	NF	X	X	X	HFBL	$$
2.26 **Paradise Cove RV Park**	TR	50	U	WES					FBL	$$$
2.27 **Preston Bend RA**	TR	40	U	WE	F, NF	X	X	X	SFBL	$$
2.28 **Walnut Creek Camp**	TR	20	40	WES	F, NF				FBL	$$
2.29 **Eisenhower SP**	TR	97	U	WES	F, NF	X	X	X	HSFBCJ	$$

Lake Texoma is a popular recreation area for campers from both Texas and Oklahoma. The lake is known as the "Striper Capital of the World" and is one of the few reservoirs in the nation where striped bass reproduce naturally. Other popular species include largemouth bass, smallmouth bass, white bass, hybrid striped bass, white crappie, black crappie, channel catfish, and blue catfish.

Lake Texoma offers a multitude of amenities for most anyone who enjoys the great outdoors. The U.S. Army Corps of Engineers offers fifteen different campgrounds, with the total number of individual campsites reaching well over 800. Also available are 40 miles of equestrian trails enjoyed by hundreds each year and the scenic Cross Timbers hiking trail, a very popular trail that winds for 14 miles above the lake on rocky ledges and through blackjack woodland.

Boat rentals, slip rentals, and supplies are available at many of the twenty-three commercial concessions located adjacent to the lake. For more information on private resorts and concessions, contact the Lake Texoma Association at (580) 564-2334.

Wildlife enthusiasts will enjoy the two national wildlife refuges located in Oklahoma and Texas. Each year thousands of Canada and snow geese, various shorebirds, several species of ducks, and bald eagles migrate to both the Hagerman and Tishomingo refuges. Deer, wild turkey, and other native animals make their home year-round on the 30,000-some acres that make up these two areas. For further information, contact Hagerman National Wildlife Refuge at (903) 786-2826 or the Tishomingo refuge at (580) 371-2402.

Eisenhower State Park, with around 423 acres, is located northwest of Denison on the shores of Lake Texoma. Campers can travel to nearby Eisenhower State Historic Site, which features the modest two-story frame house in the railroad town of Denison where Dwight D. Eisenhower was born in 1890. Eisenhower's father worked for the railroad, and the birthplace contains family possessions and period antiques demonstrating the lifestyle of a late nineteenth-century working family. The park also contains some 6 acres of scenic woods and creek bottomland intersected by an abandoned railroad track turned into a hiking path. The visitor center is a historic structure filled with hundreds of items relating to Eisenhower and his role in American and world history.

2.20 Lake Texoma–Big Mineral Camp

Location: Gordonville
Entrance fee: Day-use fee
Season: Open year-round
Camping sites: 100-plus sites, some with 30-amp electric, water, and sewer hookups; some with electric and water; and some with electric only
Maximum length: No length restrictions
Facilities: Flush toilets, dump station, WiFi
Fees per night: $$–$$$
Management: Privately owned
Contact: (903) 523-4287
Finding the campground: From Sadler, take FM 901 north about 8 miles. Watch for signs on the right side of the road.
About the campground: Both dry and wet storage are available for RVs and boats, along with a double boat ramp (small launch fee), boat rentals (pontoon, fishing, and fish/ski), and gas dock. Guide service is also available.

2.21 Lake Texoma–Cedar Mills Marina

Location: Gordonville
Entrance fee: N/A
Season: Open year-round
Camping sites: 25 RV sites with electric, water, and sewer hookups; 13 tent sites
Maximum length: No length restrictions
Facilities: Restrooms with flush toilets, showers, dump station, laundry facilities; picnic table and fire ring at each site
Fees per night: $$–$$$

Management: Privately owned
Contact: (903) 523-4222
Finding the campground: From Whitesboro, take US 377 north for approximately 11 miles. Look for signs on the right side of the road.
About the campground: Cedar Mills is located on the west end of Lake Texoma. Swimming beaches are available, along with pedal boat rentals. The boat ramp can handle craft up to 20 feet, as well as deep-keeled sailboats; a launch fee is required. There is also a fishing dock here.

2.22 Lake Texoma–Damsite Recreation Area

Location: Denison
Entrance fee: None
Season: Open year-round
Camping sites: 20 sites with electric and water hookups; 11 sites with no hookups
Maximum length: No length restrictions
Facilities: Vault toilets, showers, drinking water, dump station
Fees per night: $$
Management: U.S. Army Corps of Engineers
Contact: (903) 465-4990
Finding the campground: From Denison, take TX 91 north for 4 miles to the dam, then take FM 1310 west about 300 yards to the park entrance.
About the campground: Damsite Recreation Area is a blend of two campsites: Damsite Oklahoma and Damsite Texas. A multilane boat ramp handles boats up to 26 feet. There is also a wheelchair-accessible bank-fishing area.

2.23 Lake Texoma–Grandpappy Point Marina

Location: Denison
Entrance fee: N/A
Season: Open year-round
Camping sites: 56 sites with both full hookups and water and electric only
Maximum length: No length restrictions
Facilities: Flush toilets, dump station
Fees per night: $$–$$$
Management: Privately owned
Contact: (888) 855-1972
Finding the campground: From Denison, take US 75 north about 1 mile and turn west on TX 84. Go about 7 miles and watch for the sign.
About the campground: A boat ramp handles craft up to 20 feet. Playgrounds are also available for the kids.

2.24   Lake Texoma–Highport Marina and Resort

Location: Pottsboro
Entrance fee: N/A
Season: Open year-round
Camping sites: 15 sites with 50-amp electric, water, and sewer hookups
Maximum length: No length restrictions
Facilities: Restroom and shower facilities in boat ramp area; grill and picnic table at each site
Fees per night: $$$
Management: Privately owned
Contact: (903) 786-7000
Finding the campground: From Pottsboro, take TX 120 north approximately 5 miles to Highport Road and turn left. Highport Road will take you into the marina.
About the campground: A boat ramp (small launch fee) and boat rentals are available at the marina.

2.25   Lake Texoma–Juniper Point Recreation Area

Location: Gordonville
Entrance fee: None
Season: Open Apr through Sept
Camping sites: 40 sites with electric and water hookups; 30 sites with water only
Maximum length: No length restrictions
Facilities: Vault toilets, showers, dump station
Fees per night: $$
Management: U.S. Army Corps of Engineers
Contact: (903) 523-4022
Finding the campground: From Whitesboro, take US 377 north for about 14 miles and look for signs on the right before the lake bridge.
About the campground: Hiking and interpretive trails are available, along with two boat ramps (small launch fee).

2.26   Lake Texoma–Paradise Cove RV Park

Location: Pottsboro
Entrance fee: N/A
Season: Open year-round
Camping sites: 50 sites with electric, water, and sewer hookups
Maximum length: No length restrictions
Facilities: Besides hookups there are no facilities at this campground

Fees per night: $$$
Management: Cornerstone Marine Group
Contact: (903) 786-3890
Finding the campground: From Pottsboro, take FM 996 west about 6 miles to Locust Road and turn left. Pass a four-way stop sign about 2 miles down the road, and continue 1 mile more to the park entrance.
About the campground: The boat ramp handles boats up to 20 feet.

2.27   Lake Texoma–Preston Bend Recreation Area

Location: Pottsboro
Entrance fee: None
Season: Open Apr through Sept
Camping sites: 26 sites with electric and water hookups; 2 sites with electric only; 12 sites with water only
Maximum length: No length restrictions
Facilities: Vault and flush toilets, shower facilities, dump station
Fees per night: $$
Management: U.S. Army Corps of Engineers
Contact: (903) 786-8408
Finding the campground: From Pottsboro, take TX 120 north about 9 miles and watch for the sign on the right side of the road.
About the campground: There are two boat ramps for campers only (no launch fee required) and a swimming area. Day use is not allowed.

2.28   Walnut Creek Camp

Location: Gordonville
Entrance fee: N/A
Season: Open year-round
Camping sites: 20 sites with both full hookups and water and electric only
Maximum length: 40 feet
Facilities: Flush and vault toilets
Fees per night: $$
Management: Privately owned
Contact: (903) 523-4211
Finding the campground: From Whitesboro, take US 377 north about 12 miles, turn east on FM 901, and go 1 mile to Gordonville Road. Turn left, continue 1 mile, and look for the sign on the right.
About the campground: The ramp handles boats up to 20 feet; a small launch fee is required for non-campers.

2.29   Lake Texoma–Eisenhower State Park

Location: Denison
Entrance fee: Small fee
Season: Open year-round
Camping sites: 50 sites with electric, water, and sewer hookups; 13 premium sites with full hookups; 34 sites with water only
Maximum length: No length restrictions
Facilities: Restrooms with and without showers, dump stations; picnic table, fire ring, waist-high grill, and tent pad at premium sites
Fees per night: $$
Management: Texas Parks & Wildlife Department
Contact: (903) 465-1956
Finding the campground: The park may be reached by taking US 75 north out of Dallas for 72 miles. Exit at FM 84, turn left and travel 2 miles to Eisenhower Road. At 1.6 miles turn left on FM 1310. FM 1310 becomes Park Road 20.
About the campground: Eisenhower State Park (about 423 acres) is located in Grayson County, northwest of Denison, on the shores of Lake Texoma. The park was named for the 34th U.S. president, Dwight David Eisenhower, who was born nearby. Some of the activities here include picnicking, hiking, biking, nature study, fishing, boating (boat rentals available), waterskiing, swimming, wildlife observation, and ATV and minibike use. A fish-cleaning facility, boat-launching ramp, courtesy boat dock, lighted fishing pier, three playgrounds, and 4.5 miles of hiking and biking trails are available.

Prairies and Lakes 1

	Campsites	Total Sites	Max RV Length	Hookups	Toilets	Showers	Drinking Water	Dump Station	Recreation	Fee
2.30 Bonham SP	TR	21	U	WE	F	X	X	X	HFBLC	$$
2.31 Cleburne SP	TR	58	U	WES	F	X	X		HFC	$$-$$$
2.32 Cooper Lake–Doctors Creek RA	TR	42	U	WE	F		X		SFBLR	$$
2.33 Cooper Lake–South Sulphur Park RA	TR	117	U	WE	F		X		SFBLR	$-$$
2.34 Dinosaur Valley SP	TR	46	U	WE	F, NF	X	X	X	HC	$$-$$$
2.35 Fairfield SP	TR	181	U	WE	F, NF	X	X	X	HSFBLRC	$-$$
2.36 Lake Tawakoni SP	TR	76	U	WE	F		X	X	HSFBLC	$$
2.37 Lake Mineral Well SP & Trailway	TR	115	U	WE	F, NF	X	X	X	HSFBLRCJ	$$
2.38 Meridian SP	TR	29	U	WES	F, NF	X	X	X	HSFBLC	$$-$$$
2.39 Purtis Creek SP	TR	78	U	WE	F, NF		X		HFBLCJ	$-$$
2.40 Ray Roberts Lake–Isle du Bois SP	TR	182	U	WE	F, NF		X	X	HSFBLRC	$$-$$$
2.41 Ray Roberts Lake–Johnson Branch SP	TR	187	U	WE	F, NF		X		HSFBLRC	$-$$$

Campgrounds in the prairies and lakes region offer a wide range of camping opportunities, from walk-in primitive campsites to modern RV pads with all the amenities. Each campground has its own personality.

Popular destinations within this area include the two state parks on Ray Roberts Lake: Isle du Bois and Johnson Branch. These state parks, along with six satellite parks (Jordan Unit, Pond Creek, Pecan Creek, Buck Creek, Sanger, and Elm Fork), wildlife management areas, wetlands, waterfowl sanctuaries, and the 20-mile Ray Roberts Lake/Lake Lewisville Greenbelt Corridor, offer bird-watching, water sports, horseback riding, hiking, or backpacking along scenic trails. Dinosaur Valley State Park in Glen Rose offers campers an up-close look at what dinosaurs may have been like in prehistoric days. The park contains some of the best-preserved dinosaur tracks in the world, in addition to fiberglass models of an apatosaurus and Tyrannosaurus rex.

From great fishing and boating at Cooper Lake, Fairfield Lake, Purtis Creek, and Ray Roberts Lake, this area offers a lot for campers to enjoy.

2.30   Bonham State Park

Location: Bonham
Entrance fee: Small fee
Season: Open year-round
Camping sites: 21 sites with electric and water hookups, 7 of which are tent-only
Maximum length: No length restrictions
Facilities: Restrooms with and without showers, dump station
Fees per night: $$
Management: Texas Parks & Wildlife Department
Contact: (903) 583-5022
Finding the campground: From Bonham, take TX 78 southeast for 1.5 miles to FM 271. Travel 2 miles southeast on FM 271, and enter on Park Road 24.
About the campground: Bonham State Park is a 261-acre park located in Fannin County northeast of Dallas. It includes a 65-acre lake, rolling prairies, and woodlands; picnic sites (including a group picnic area); an 11-mile trail for mountain biking and hiking; a playground; a boat ramp and dock; and a lighted fishing pier.

2.31   Cleburne State Park

Location: Cleburne
Entrance fee: Small fee
Season: Open year-round
Camping sites: 31 sites with electric and water hookups; 27 sites with electric, water, and sewer hookups
Maximum length: No length restrictions
Facilities: Picnic table, grill, and campfire ring at each site; restrooms with hot showers nearby
Fees per night: $$–$$$
Management: Texas Parks & Wildlife Department
Contact: (817) 645-4215
Finding the campground: From Cleburne, take US 67 south 8.5 miles and turn left on Park Road 21. The park is another 6 miles on the right.
About the campground: Cleburne is a 528-acre state park that encompasses a 116-acre spring-fed lake, located southwest of Fort Worth in Johnson County. The park's mountain bike trails offer 5.5 miles of beautiful scenery with a variety of challenges for all experience levels.

2.32 Cooper Lake State Park– Doctors Creek Recreation Area

Location: Cooper
Entrance fee: Small fee
Season: Open year-round
Camping sites: 42 sites with electric and water hookups
Maximum length: No length restrictions
Facilities: Flush toilets; picnic table, fire ring, and BBQ grill at each site
Fees per night: $$
Management: Texas Parks & Wildlife Department
Contact: (903) 395-3100
Finding the campground: From Cooper, take TX 154 east for 1 mile, then go south for 2 miles on FM 1529 to the park entrance; or from I-30, exit 122, on the west side of Sulphur Springs, take TX 19 north for 14 miles, then CR 4795 west for 2 miles, to the U.S Army Corps of Engineers office, cross the lake dam, and drive 0.5 mile farther to the park entrance.
About the campground: Doctors Creek Unit (715.5 acres) is located in Delta County. The rolling hills of Cooper Lake State Park offer spectacular views of Cooper Lake. The park is centrally located to surrounding communities, including Paris, Cooper, Greenville, Sulphur Springs, and Commerce, as well as the urban centers of Dallas/Fort Worth and Texarkana. Activities include fishing, waterskiing, picnicking, boating, unsupervised swimming, bird-watching, nature study, educational programs, and tours. There is a three-lane boat ramp and fish-cleaning table. The South Sulphur Unit also offers equestrian camping and horseback-riding trails.

2.33 Cooper Lake State Park– South Sulphur Recreation Area

Location: Sulphur Springs
Entrance fee: Small fee
Season: Open year-round
Camping sites: 87 sites with electric and water hookups; 15 equestrian sites with electric and water hookups; 15 walk-in sites
Maximum length: No length restrictions
Facilities: Flush toilets, picnic tables, fire rings, lantern poles
Fees per night: $–$$
Management: Texas Parks & Wildlife Department
Contact: (903) 945-5256

Finding the campground: From I-30, exit 122, on the west side of Sulphur Springs, travel north 10 miles on TX 19, west 4 miles on TX 71, and then north 1 mile on FM 3505 to the park entrance; or from Cooper, go east 1 mile on TX 154, south 5 miles on FM 1529 (cross the lake dam), south 5 miles on TX 19, west 4 miles on TX 71, and then north 1 mile on FM 3505 to the park entrance.

About the campground: South Sulphur Unit (2,310.5 acres) is located in northern Hopkins County. The rolling hills of Cooper Lake State Park offer spectacular views of Cooper Lake. The South Sulphur Recreation Area has two lighted fishing piers, two boat ramps, three picnic areas, a group pavilion, a playground, a 5 mile hike/bike trail, a 10.5 mile equestrian trail, an outdoor amphitheater, a sand volleyball court, and a large sandy swimming beach. The park is centrally located to surrounding communities, including Paris, Cooper, Greenville, Sulphur Springs, and Commerce, as well as the urban centers of Dallas/Fort Worth and Texarkana.

2.34   Dinosaur Valley State Park

Location: Glen Rose
Entrance fee: Small fee
Season: Open year-round
Camping sites: 46 sites with electric and water hookups; primitive backpacking sites (1- to 2.5-mile hike in)
Maximum length: No length restrictions
Facilities: Restrooms with showers, dump station, picnic tables, fire rings and/or grills; backpacking sites have water available at the trailhead
Fees per night: $$–$$$
Management: Texas Parks & Wildlife Department
Contact: (254) 897-4588
Finding the campground: The park is located 4 miles west of Glen Rose. Take US 67 from Glen Rose to FM 205 for 4 miles to Park Road 59, then go 1 mile to the headquarters.
About the campground: Dinosaur Valley State Park, located just northwest of Glen Rose in Somervell County, is a 1,525-acre scenic park set astride the Paluxy River. The park contains some of the best-preserved dinosaur tracks in the world. The tracks are located in the riverbed, so please call ahead to check on river conditions. There are two fiberglass models: a 70-foot apatosaurus and a 45-foot Tyrannosaurus rex. Twelve miles of hiking and biking trails are also available.

2.35   Fairfield State Park

Location: Fairfield
Entrance fee: Small fee
Season: Open year-round, except during public hunts
Camping sites: 96 sites with electric and water hookups (35 closed Dec–Feb); 35 sites with water only (closed Dec–Feb); 50 hike-in primitive sites (closed Dec–Feb)
Maximum length: No length restrictions
Facilities: Restrooms with and without showers, dump station, picnic tables, fire rings and/or grills
Fees per night: $–$$
Management: Texas Parks & Wildlife Department
Contact: (903) 389-4514
Finding the campground: The park is 6 miles northeast of Fairfield off FM 2570 on FM 3285. From Fairfield travel east on US 84 1.8 miles to FM 488. Take FM 488 northeast to FM 2570 traveling 0.7 mile to State Park Road 64.
About the campground: Fairfield State Park consists of 1,460 acres northeast of the city of Fairfield in Freestone County, just a few miles from I-45. Activities include backpacking, hiking, horseback riding, nature study, bird-watching, boating on this 2,400-acre lake, waterskiing, jet skiing, fishing, and lake swimming in a large, buoyed, sandy area. A lighted fishing pier, fish-cleaning shelter and table, boat ramps, and playgrounds are available.

2.36   Lake Tawakoni State Park

Location: Wills Point
Entrance fee: Small fee
Season: Open year-round
Camping sites: 76 sites with electric and water hookups
Maximum length: No length restrictions
Facilities: Flush toilets, dump station; 18-by-40-foot canopy tent available for rent (contact park for details)
Fees per night: $$
Management: Texas Parks & Wildlife Department
Contact: (903) 560-7123
Finding the campground: Exit from I-20 at TX 47. Go north on TX 47 about 10 miles take TX 47 north through Wills Point to FM 2475, then continue for about 4 miles to the park entrance.
About the campground: Lake Tawakoni State Park is a 376-acre park in Hunt County, about 50 miles east of Dallas, with 5.2 miles of shoreline along the south-central main body of the reservoir. With a total shoreline of about 200 miles, stretching through Hunt, Rains, and Van Zandt Counties, Lake Tawakoni provides water-oriented recreation for much of central northeast Texas. Activities include picnicking, boating (four-lane ramp available), swimming, fishing, hiking (5.5 miles of trails), and mountain biking.

2.37   Lake Mineral Wells State Park and Trailway

Location: Mineral Wells
Entrance fee: Small fee
Season: Open year-round, except during public hunts
Camping sites: 64 sites with electric and water hookups; 11 sites with water only; 20 hike-in primitive sites; 20 equestrian sites with water
Maximum length: No length restrictions
Facilities: Restrooms with showers, picnic tables, grills, dump station
Fees per night: $$
Management: Texas Parks & Wildlife Department
Contact: (940) 328-1171
Finding the campground: From Weatherford, take US 180 14 miles west to the park entrance.
About the campground: Lake Mineral Wells State Park, located 4 miles east of Mineral Wells in Parker County, consists of 3,282.5 acres and encompasses Lake Mineral Wells. Activities include swimming; fishing; boating (boat, canoe, and paddleboat rentals; no skiing, personal watercraft, or tubing permitted); rock climbing; mountain biking; hiking; and horseback riding (visitors must provide their own horses). A boat ramp and fishing pier are available.

2.38   Meridian State Park

Location: Meridian
Entrance fee: Small fee
Season: Open year-round
Camping sites: 6 developed drive-up sites; 8 developed drive-up sites with water; 7 sites with electric and water hookups; 8 sites with sewer, electric, and water hookups
Maximum length: No length restrictions
Facilities: Restrooms with showers, dump station
Fees per night: $$–$$$
Management: Texas Parks & Wildlife Department
Contact: (254) 435-2536
Finding the campground: From Meridian, take TX 22 southwest for about 3 miles to the park entrance.
About the campground: Hidden away in the wooded hills northwest of Waco is Meridian State Park, a haven for nature lovers and fishing enthusiasts. In addition to fishing, the park's 72-acre lake offers swimming and no-wake boating (boat dock and ramp available). A hiking trail encircles Lake Meridian and features limestone outcroppings with fossils, a scenic overlook, and aquatic vegetation. Bird-watching is excellent, with a good chance of seeing the rare golden-cheeked warbler. Other activities include picnicking and bicycling or scenic driving on 5 miles of paved park road.

2.39 Purtis Creek State Park

Location: Eustace
Entrance fee: Small fee
Season: Open year-round
Camping sites: 59 sites with electric and water hookups; 14 primitive hike-in (0.65 mile) sites; 5 walk-in (10–15 yards) sites
Maximum length: No length restrictions
Facilities: Flush and vault toilets, drinking water
Fees per night: $–$$
Management: Texas Parks & Wildlife Department
Contact: (903) 425-2332
Finding the campground: From Athens, take US 175 west for 12 miles to Eustace, then go right (north) on FM 316 for 3.5 miles.
About the campground: Purtis Creek State Park is located in Henderson and Van Zandt Counties and has a total acreage of about 1,582. Activities include picnicking, fishing, boating, and hiking. The park rents paddleboats, kayaks, and canoes. Lighted fishing piers, fish-cleaning shelters, boat ramps, courtesy docks, and a playground are also available.

2.40 Ray Roberts Lake–Isle du Bois State Park

Location: Pilot Point
Entrance fee: Small fee
Season: Open year-round
Camping Sites: 115 sites with electric (102 with 30-amp, 13 with 50-amp) and water hookups; 53 walk-in (0.125–0.25 mile) developed tent sites; 14 equestrian sites with water
Maximum length: No length restrictions
Facilities: Restrooms with flush toilets, dump station; sites with hookups have a picnic table and fire ring and/or grill; walk-in sites have a picnic table, tent pad, fire ring, lamp post, and water in the area; equestrian sites have a picnic table, fire ring and/or grill, hitching/tethering posts, and water in the area.
Fees per night: $$–$$$
Management: Texas Parks & Wildlife Department
Contact: (940) 686-2148
Finding the campground: From Denton go north on I-35, 10 miles, exit at FM 455 and proceed east 10 miles. The park is located on FM 455, 10 miles east of I-35.
About the campground: Situated along the shores of a 30,000-acre reservoir, the Ray Roberts Lake State Park complex consists of two park units (Isle du Bois and Johnson Branch), six satellite parks (Jordan Unit, Pond Creek, Pecan Creek, Buck Creek, Sanger, and Elm Fork), wildlife management areas, wetlands, waterfowl sanctuaries, and the 20-mile Ray Roberts Lake/Lake Lewisville Greenbelt Corridor. With picnicking, mountain biking, inline skating, swimming, boating, fishing, bird-watching, horseback riding, and hiking or backpacking along a scenic trail, Ray Roberts has something for everyone.

2.41　Ray Roberts Lake–Johnson Branch State Park

Location: Valley View

Entrance fee: Small fee

Season: Open year-round

Camping sites: 104 sites with electric and water hookups; 50 walk-in (0.25 mile) developed tent sites; 33 hike-in primitive sites

Maximum length: No length restrictions

Facilities: Restrooms with flush toilets, picnic tables, fire rings, grills, lantern holders

Fees per night: $–$$$

Management: Texas Parks & Wildlife Department

Contact: (940) 637-2294

Finding the campground: From Dallas take I-35 north through Sanger and into Valley View, exiting at exit 483 leading to FM 3002. The park is located on FM 3002, 7 miles east of I-35.

About the campground: Situated along the shores of a 30,000-acre reservoir, the Ray Roberts Lake State Park complex consists of two park units (Isle du Bois and Johnson Branch), six satellite parks (Jordan Unit, Pond Creek, Pecan Creek, Buck Creek, Sanger, and Elm Fork), wildlife management areas, wetlands, waterfowl sanctuaries, and the 20-mile Ray Roberts Lake/Lake Lewisville Greenbelt Corridor. With picnicking, mountain biking, inline skating, swimming, boating, fishing, bird-watching, horseback riding, and hiking or backpacking along a scenic trail, Ray Roberts has something for everyone.

Grapevine, Joe Pool, and Lewisville Lakes

		Campsites	Total Sites	Max RV Length	Hookups	Toilets	Showers	Drinking Water	Dump Station	Recreation	Fee
2.42	Grapevine Lake—Twin Coves RA	TR	47	U	WE	F, NF	X	X	X	FBLC	$$$
2.43	Grapevine Lake—Murrell RA	T	36	N/A		F, NF	X			HFBL	
2.44	Grapevine Lake—Vineyards Campground	TR	62	U	WESI	F	X	X		FBL	$$$
2.45	Joe Pool Lake—Cedar Hill SP	TR	385	U	WE	F, NF	X	X	X	HFBLCJ	$-$$$
2.46	Joe Pool Lake—Loyd RA	TR	221	U	WE	F	X	X		FBL	$$
2.47	Lake Lewisville—Hickory Creek RA	TR	136	U	WE	F, NF	X	X	X	HFBLC	$$
2.48	Lake Lewisville—Pilot Knoll RA	TR	57	U	WE	F	X	X	X	HSFBL	$$-$$$

Grapevine Lake, a U.S. Army Corps of Engineers reservoir located in the heart of the Dallas/Fort Worth metroplex, offers camping, multiuse trails, water recreation, picnic facilities, pavilions for large gatherings, hunting, and much more. Grapevine is a popular spot for sailboating and windsurfing as well. Murrell Park offers sites for tent and primitive camping, and the park's boat ramps allow for easy access to the water from the north side of the lake. Grapevine also has two lessee-operated campgrounds, Twin Coves and The Vineyards.

Cedar Hill State Park, a Texas Parks & Wildlife Department park, has one of the larger campgrounds in the area, offering 385 sites. The park is described by Texas Parks & Wildlife as an "urban nature preserve" located on the 7,500-acre Joe Pool Reservoir. Cedar Hill's proximity to major metropolitan areas makes it an ideal destination for families who want to enjoy the great outdoors without spending precious time driving.

Lake Lewisville is a large reservoir (29,592-acres) located on the Elm Fork of the Trinity River near Lewisville, just north of Dallas off I-35.

2.42 Grapevine Lake–Twin Coves Recreation Area

Location: Flower Mound
Entrance fee: None
Season: Open year-round
Camping sites: 43 RV sites with 30-amp electric and water hookups; 4 tent sites
Maximum length: No length restrictions
Facilities: Restrooms with showers, 2 dump stations, fire rings, covered picnic tables
Fees per night: $$$
Management: Marinas International
Contact: (972) 539-1030
Finding the campground: From the intersection of TX 31 and FM 709 in Dawson, travel 4 miles north on FM 709 to the park entrance.
About the campground: Twin Coves is surrounded on two sides by Grapevine Lake, providing good fishing access. Hiking and mountain biking trails are available, along with a fish-cleaning station, fishing dock, playground, and volleyball court.

2.43 Grapevine Lake–Murrell Recreation Area

Location: Flower Mound
Entrance fee: None
Season: Open year-round
Camping sites: 36 tent sites
Maximum length: N/A
Facilities: Restrooms, grills, fire rings, covered picnic tables
Fees per night: None
Management: U.S. Army Corps of Engineers
Contact: (469) 645-9100
Finding the campground: Going north on I-35 from Ft. Worth about 24 miles, exit on FM 1171. Turn right and travel about 10 miles. The park is located on the north side of Grapevine Lake, at the end of Simmons Road (also known as Whites Chapel Road) in Flower Mound, which is easily accessed from FM 2499.
About the campground: Murrell has access to the Northshore Trail (trailhead has a covered rest area and water fountain) and the Twin Coves Marina. The park also has two boat ramps and several fishing trails for added shoreline access.

2.44 Grapevine Lake–Vineyards Campground

Location: Flower Mound
Entrance fee: None
Season: Open year-round
Camping sites: 62 RV sites with electric and water hookups (some with sewer) and tent sites
Maximum length: No length restrictions
Facilities: Restrooms with showers, laundry room, WiFi
Fees per night: $$$
Management: City of Grapevine
Contact: (817) 329-8993
Finding the campground: From Ft. Worth travel north on I-35E, exiting at exit 52B, take TX 121 south 11 miles and exit at TX 26 south to N. Dooley Street Travel 3.1 miles, then turn right for 1 mile to the campground entrance on the left at 1501 N. Dooley St.
About the campground: The Vineyards is located in the heart of the metroplex and everything is close, from the Stockyards of Fort Worth to the West End in Dallas. Courtesy docks, a boat ramp, and a fishing pier are available.

2.45 Joe Pool Lake–Cedar Hill State Park

Location: Cedar Hill
Entrance fee: Small fee
Season: Open year-round
Camping sites: 355 sites with electric and water hookups; 30 hike-in (0.25 mile minimum) primitive sites
Maximum length: No length restrictions
Facilities: Fire ring, lantern pole, and picnic table at each site; restrooms with hot showers; 2 dump stations; group picnic pavilions (capacities 50 and 100)
Fees per night: $–$$$
Management: Texas Parks & Wildlife Department
Contact: (972) 291-3900
Finding the campground: The park is located 10 miles southwest of Dallas and 3 miles west of Cedar Hill. From US 67, exit at FM 1382 and travel 2.5 miles north to the park entrance on the left. From I-20, exit at FM 1382 and travel 4 miles south to the park entrance on the right. The park is skirted by FM 1382 and Mansfield Road.
About the campground: Cedar Hill Park features 355 developed, mostly wooded campsites with a shade shelter over some of the picnic tables. Additionally, there are 30 primitive, nonreservable campsites. These sites are not near water, but a composting toilet is in the area; campfires are not permitted.

The park is home to the premier north Texas mountain bike trail. The DORBA trail, named for the volunteers of the Dallas Off Road Biking Association, was built by mountain bikers for mountain bikers. Over 1,200 acres of prime mountain bike landscape are crisscrossed with 15 miles of intense riding. Cedar Hill also has 4.5 miles of hiking/backpacking trails. Bird-watching is a popular year-round activity, as is lake fishing for largemouth bass, crappie, and catfish. The park features two lighted fishing jetties and a perch pond for youngsters.

Joe Pool Marina (972-299-9010) rents ski boats, paddleboats, personal watercraft, pontoon boats, and a houseboat for family activities; yearly boat slip rentals are available. They also have an indoor/outdoor fishing barge, and two concrete four-lane boat ramps welcome the boating enthusiast. The marina's store sells bait, fishing and camping gear, and food products.

2.46 Joe Pool Lake–Loyd Recreation Area

Location: Grand Prairie
Entrance fee: Small fee
Season: Open year-round
Camping sites: 221 sites with water and 30-amp electric hookups
Maximum length: No length restrictions
Facilities: Restrooms with showers, picnic areas
Fees per night: $$, plus entrance fee
Management: City of Grand Prairie
Contact: (817) 467-2104
Finding the campground: The park is located on the northwest side of Joe Pool Lake, east of SH 360 off Ragland Road.
About the campground: Campers at 791-acre Loyd Park enjoy a tranquil, natural, tree-filled setting located in the heart of the Dallas/Fort Worth metroplex. The park has playgrounds, boat docks, and a four-lane boat ramp.

2.47 Lake Lewisville–Hickory Creek Recreation Area

Location: Hickory Creek
Entrance fee: Included in camping fee (entry restricted to campers)
Season: Open year-round
Camping sites: 126 sites with water and electric hookups; 10 primitive sites
Maximum length: No length restrictions
Facilities: Restrooms with showers, dump station; picnic tables, fire rings, and grills at hookup sites
Fees per day: $$
Management: U.S. Army Corps of Engineers
Contact: (469) 645-9100

Finding the campground: The park is located off I-35E. Exit at FM 2181/Swisher Road (exit 458), turn right onto Turbeville Road, then turn left onto Point Vista Road. The park will be on your right. Hickory Creek is located close to restaurants, a movie theater, and grocery shopping.

About the campground: Hickory Creek Recreation Area provides shoreline access for fishing, a swimming beach, a boat ramp, walking and biking trails, and playgrounds.

2.48 Lake Lewisville–Pilot Knoll Recreation Area

Location: Highland Village
Entrance fee: Small fee
Season: Open year-round
Camping sites: 48 sites with 30-amp electric and water hookups; 9 sites with 50-amp electric and water hookups
Maximum length: No length restrictions
Facilities: Restroom with showers, dump station; grill, picnic table, and fire ring at each site
Fees per night: $$–$$$
Management: Highland Village
Contact: (940) 455-2228
Finding the campground: The park is located off of FM 407 and Chinn Chapel Road.
About the campground: Pilot Knoll Park is located on the western edge of Lake Lewisville, outside of Dallas. In addition to camping, visitors to the lake enjoy picnicking, swimming, boating, fishing, and relaxing in the great outdoors. Amenities include a boat launch, day-use group shelters, a playground, and a short nature trail. Attendants are on duty from 6:00 a.m. to 10:00 p.m.

Navarro Mills Lake

	Campsites	Total Sites	Max RV Length	Hookups	Toilets	Showers	Drinking Water	Dump Station	Recreation	Fee
2.49 Liberty Hill Park	TR	102	U	WES	F	X	X	X	HSFBLC	$$-$$$
2.50 Oak Park	TR	48	U	WES	F	X	X	X	HSFBL	$$-$$$
2.51 Pecan Point	TR	35	U	WE	F	X	X	X	F	$-$$
2.52 Wolf Creek Park	TR	72	U	WE	F	X	X	X	HFBL	$$

Navarro Mills is located 16 miles west of Corsicana and offers 5,060 acres of fishing, camping, hunting, boating, hiking, and other activities in parks and other public lands. The U.S. Army Corps of Engineers operates four public access areas with boat ramps. A marina at Liberty Hill Park offers bait, supplies, and boat rentals.

Navarro Mills Lake holds the Texas state record for the largest white crappie and is one of the best crappie lakes in Texas. Catfish and crappie anglers will find live bait works best in the inundated timber in the lake's upper end.

2.49   Navarro Mills Lake–Liberty Hill Park

Location: Corsicana
Entrance fee: None
Season: Open year-round
Camping sites: 99 sites with water and electric hookups (3 are screened shelters and 6 also have sewer hookups); 3 sites with no hookups
Maximum length: No length restrictions
Facilities: Restrooms with flush toilets and showers, dump station, picnic areas
Fees per night: $$-$$$
Management: U.S. Army Corps of Engineers
Contact: (254) 578-1431
Finding the campground: From Corsicana, take TX 31, 21 miles to Dawson, turn north onto FM 709, and travel about 4 miles to the park entrance.

About the campground: Navarro Mills Lake is described as the best-kept secret of the Fort Worth District of the Army Corps of Engineers. Liberty Hill Park is located on the southern shore of Navarro Mills. The lake holds the current state record for white crappie, and anglers come from all over to sample some of the best crappie fishing anywhere. In addition to fishing, Navarro Mills offers 5,060 acres of hunting, boating, hiking, and other activities available in parks and other public lands. There are fishing piers in Liberty Hill, Oak, and Wolf Creek Parks, and no fee is charged for their use. Other amenities include two boat ramps (small launch fee), a playground, and a swimming beach. The Navarro Mills Lake Marina (254-578-1131), located in Liberty Hill Park, sells a wide assortment of supplies for boaters, anglers, picnickers, and campers. Hunting and fishing licenses are also sold at the store.

2.50   Navarro Mills Lake–Oak Park

Location: Corsicana
Entrance fee: None
Season: Open year-round
Camping sites: 48 sites with 30-amp electric and water hookups (some sites also have sewer hookups)
Maximum length: No length restrictions
Facilities: Restrooms with flush toilets and showers, dump station, picnic areas
Fees per night: $$–$$$
Management: U.S. Army Corps of Engineers
Contact: (254) 578-1431
Finding the campground: From Corsicana, travel approximately 20 miles west on TX 31. At the intersection with FM 667 turn north (right) and travel about 1.5 miles to arrive at the Navarro Mills Lake Office, which will be on the left (west) side of the road.
About the campground: Oak Park is located on the northeastern shore of Navarro Mills Lake. The lake holds the current state record for white crappie, and anglers come from all over to sample some of the best crappie fishing anywhere. In addition to fishing, Navarro Mills offers 5,060 acres of hunting, boating, hiking, and other activities. The Alliance Creek Nature Trail is a 0.5-mile path through a heavily wooded area in Oak Park. The trail describes interesting features of the area, such as native trees, shrubs, and vines, and is a nonstrenuous fifteen-minute walk. A designated swimming area, playground, fishing pier, and boat ramp (small launch fee) are also available.

2.51 Navarro Mills Lake–Pecan Point

Location: Corsicana
Entrance fee: None
Season: Open Apr through Sept
Camping sites: 5 sites with 50-amp electric and water hookups service; 30 sites without hookups
Maximum length: No length restrictions
Facilities: Restrooms with flush toilets and showers, dump station
Fees per night: $-$$
Management: U.S. Army Corps of Engineers
Contact: (254) 578-1431
Finding the campground: From Corsicana, take TX 31 southwest for 20 miles, then FM 667 north for 1 mile.
About the campground: Pecan Point Park is located on the north shore of Navarro Mills Lake, with some of the best crappie fishing in Texas.

2.52 Navarro Mills Lake–Wolf Creek Park

Location: Corsicana
Entrance fee: None
Season: Open Apr through Sept
Camping sites: 50 sites with water and electric hookups; 22 sites without hookups (2 are double sites)
Maximum length: No length restrictions
Facilities: Restrooms with flush toilets and showers, dump station
Fees per night: $$
Management: U.S. Army Corps of Engineers
Contact: (254) 578-1431
Finding the campground: From the intersection of TX 31 and FM 667, travel about 3 miles north on FM 667 to FM 639. Turn west (left) on FM 639 and go about 2 miles to Wolf Creek Park (FM 639 ends at the park entrance).
About the campground: Wolf Creek Park is located on the north shore of Navarro Mills Lake, which offers fishing, hunting, boating, hiking, and other activities There are fishing piers in Liberty Hill, Oak, and Wolf Creek Parks, and no fee is charged for their use. A two-lane boat ramp (small launch fee) with a courtesy dock is also available.

Lake Whitney

		Campsites	Total Sites	Max RV Length	Hookups	Toilets	Showers	Drinking Water	Dump Station	Recreation	Fee
2.53	Cedar Creek RA	TR	20	U	E	F		X		FBL	
2.54	Cedron Creek RA	TR	57	U	WE	F	X	X	X	FBL	$$
2.55	Juniper Cove Marina	TR	100	45	WE	F	X	X	X	FBL	$$$
2.56	Kimball Bend RA	T	12	N/A		NF				FBL	
2.57	East Lofers Bend RA	TR	66	U	WE	F	X	X	X	FBL	$$
2.58	West Lofers Bend RA	TR	68	U	WE	F	X	X	X	FBL	$$-$$$
2.59	McCown Valley RA	TR	52	U	WE	F	X	X	X	SFBLR	$$-$$$
2.60	Plowman Creek RA	TR	34	U	WE	F	X	X	X	FBL	$$
2.61	Riverside RA	T	5	N/A		NF				F	
2.62	Soldiers Bluff RA	T	14	N/A	W	NF		X		F	
2.63	Lake Whitney SP	TR	137	U	WES	F	X	X	X	HSFBLC	$-$$

Lake Whitney, 23,500 surface acres, is located on the main stem of the Brazos River, about 30 miles north of Waco and 65 miles southwest of Fort Worth. Whitney is one of the prettiest lakes in Texas. This, combined with excellent public access and good fishing for many species, makes it a popular destination. The lake offers top-notch angling for striped bass and white bass, along with unique and diverse opportunities for smallmouth bass and trophy blue catfish. Its reputation as a hot spot for bass is a big draw for fishing enthusiasts from around the country.

The Lake Whitney area also boasts three public 18-hole golf courses and thousands of acres of winding trails for horseback riding. Bird and wildlife enthusiasts enjoy the area's 300 migratory and nonmigratory birds and a local wildlife population that features over 50 different species, including white-tailed deer and turkey.

2.53 Lake Whitney–Cedar Creek Recreation Area

Location: Clifton
Entrance fee: None
Season: Open year-round
Camping sites: 20 sites, both with and without electric hookups
Maximum length: No length restrictions
Facilities: Restrooms with flush toilets, drinking water, ground cookers/fire rings
Fees per night: None
Management: U.S. Army Corps of Engineers
Contact: (254) 622-3332
Finding the campground: From Whitney Lake Dam, take TX 22 east 5.5 miles to the city of Whitney. Take FM 993 north about 5 or 6 miles, turn left on CR 2604, then turn left at the Cedar Creek park sign.
About the campground: Cedar Creek Recreation Area is located on the east side of Whitney Lake and offers free camping, picnicking, and boat-launching facilities (double-lane ramp).

2.54 Lake Whitney–Cedron Creek Recreation Area

Location: Clifton
Entrance fee: None
Season: Campground usually open Apr through Sept
Camping sites: 57 sites with 30- or 50-amp electric and water hookups
Maximum length: No length restrictions
Facilities: Restrooms with showers, dump station; upright BBQ and ground cooker/fire ring at each site
Fees per night: $$
Management: U.S. Army Corps of Engineers
Contact: (254) 622-3332
Finding the campground: From I-35 in Hillsboro, take TX 22 west for 12 miles to Whitney. From Whitney, take TX 933 north for 3 miles, turn left on FM 1713, and cross the bridge over the lake. Cedron will be the first road on the left; follow signs to the campground.
About the campground: Cedron Creek Campground is located at Whitney Lake on the main stem of the Brazos River. The park is on the west side, approximately halfway up the lake on FM 1713, and features horseshoes pits and a double-lane boat ramp. People not camping (or visiting someone who is camping) in the park must pay a small fee to use the ramp.

2.55 Lake Whitney–Juniper Cove Marina

Location: Whitney
Entrance fee: None
Season: Open year-round
Camping sites: 100 sites with electric and water hookups
Maximum length: 45 feet
Facilities: Restrooms with showers, dump station, covered and uncovered picnic tables
Fees per night: $$$
Management: Lake Whitney Marina at Juniper Cove
Contact: (254) 694-3129
Finding the campground: Coming from Hillsboro on I-35, take 368A exit and follow the signs to Whitney. At the Whitney city limits keep to the right onto Texas 180 Spur and follow the signs to Blum. At the traffic signal turn right on to FM 933 North. Turn left on to FM 1713. Turn right on Juniper Cove Road.
About the campground: Juniper Cove is a full-service marina on Lake Whitney. The marina offers lakefront cabins in addition to its shaded campground. Vessels up to 80 feet and RVs up to 45 feet can be accommodated. Amenities and services include wet slips, a boat launch, ship's store, and gas. Those not camping at the marina must pay a small fee for the boat launch and fishing barge.

2.56 Lake Whitney–Kimball Bend Recreation Area

Location: Blum
Entrance fee: No fee
Season: Open year-round
Camping sites: 12 tent sites
Maximum length: N/A
Facilities: Vault toilets
Fees per night: No fee
Management: U.S. Army Corps of Engineers
Contact: (254) 694-3189
Finding the campground: From Cleburne, travel South on TX 174 for approximately 22 miles. Turn right into Kimball Bend Park after you cross the TX 174 Bridge.
About the campground: Kimball Bend Recreation Area is on the site of the original low-water fording of the Brazos River as early settlers moved west. A boat ramp is available.

2.57 Lake Whitney–East Lofers Bend Recreation Area

Location: Whitney
Entrance fee: None
Season: Open year-round
Camping sites: 60 sites with 30-amp electric and water hookups; 6 sites with water only
Maximum length: No length restrictions
Facilities: Restrooms with showers, dump station; upright BBQ and ground cooker/fire ring at each site
Fees per night: $$
Management: U.S. Army Corps of Engineers
Contact: (254) 694-3189
Finding the campground: From I-35 in Hillsboro, take TX 22 W, 12 miles to Whitney, continue 7 miles, past Whitney, turn right before dam. Follow Park Road to 4 way stop. Turn right to go to East Lofers to the gate house on TX 22.
About the campground: East Lofers Bend Recreation Area has two boat ramps: One is a double-lane ramp with adequate parking, and the other is a shallow, single-lane ramp. People not camping (or visiting someone who is camping) in the park must pay a small fee to use the boat ramps.

2.58 Lake Whitney–West Lofers Bend Recreation Area

Location: Whitney
Entrance fee: None
Season: Usually open Apr through Sept
Camping sites: 40 sites with 30-amp electric and water hookups; 6 sites with 50-amp electric and water hookups; 22 sites with water only
Maximum length: No length restrictions
Facilities: Restrooms with showers, dump station; upright BBQ and ground cooker/fire ring at each site
Fees per night: $$–$$$
Management: U.S. Army Corps of Engineers
Contact: (254) 694-3189
Finding the campground: From I-35 in Hillsboro, take TX 22 W, 12 miles to Whitney, continue 7 miles, past Whitney, turn right before dam. Follow Park Road to 4 way stop. Turn left to go to West Lofers on TX 22. The main entrance to West Lofers Bend is located on the east end of the Whitney Dam on TX 22. After turning into the main entrance, follow the signs to the park.
About the campground: People not camping (or visiting someone who is camping) in the park must pay a small fee to use the boat ramp.

2.59 Lake Whitney–McCown Valley Recreation Area

Location: Whitney
Entrance fee: None
Season: Open year-round
Camping sites: 31 sites with water and 30-amp electric hookups; 14 sites with water and 50-amp electric hookups; 7 sites with water only
Maximum length: No length restrictions
Facilities: Restrooms with showers, dump station; upright BBQ and ground cooker/fire ring at each site; equestrian camping area; 5 cabins available for rent
Fees per night: $$–$$$
Management: U.S. Army Corps of Engineers
Contact: (254) 694-3189
Finding the campground: From I-35, exit at TX 22 in Hillsboro and take TX 22 west for 12 miles to Whitney. Take TX 933 north for 2.5 miles to FM 1713 and proceed 6 miles west, following signs to the campground.
About the campground: McCown Valley Recreation Area is located on the east side of Lake Whitney, approximately halfway up the lake. The park features horseshoes pits and a large three-lane boat ramp, along with one of the two swimming beaches on the lake. People not camping (or visiting someone who is camping) in the park must pay a small fee to use the boat ramp.

2.60   Lake Whitney–Plowman Creek Recreation Area

Location: Kopperl
Entrance fee: None
Season: Open year-round
Camping sites: 22 sites with water and 30-amp electric hookups; 12 sites with water only
Maximum length: No length restrictions
Facilities: Restrooms with showers, dump station; upright BBQ and ground cooker/fire ring at each site
Fees per night: $$
Management: U.S. Army Corps of Engineers
Contact: (254) 694-3189
Finding the campground: From Kopperl, travel 1 mile south on FM 56, following signs to the campground.
About the campground: Plowman Creek Recreation Area is located on the west side of the lake. The campground requires a two-day minimum stay on weekends. People not camping (or visiting someone who is camping) in the park must pay a small fee to use the boat ramp.

2.61   Lake Whitney–Riverside Recreation Area

Location: Downstream of the Whitney Dam
Entrance fee: None
Season: Open year-round
Camping sites: 5 tent-only picnic/camping sites (access road is closed when floodwater is being released)
Maximum length: N/A
Facilities: Toilets
Fees per night: None
Management: U.S. Army Corps of Engineers
Contact: (254) 694-3189
Finding the campground: Riverside Recreation Area is located downstream of the Whitney Dam.
About the campground: The park has a fishing platform, and there is a gravel access road on the east side of the river.

2.62 Lake Whitney–Soldiers Bluff Recreation Area

Location: Clifton
Entrance fee: None
Season: Open year-round
Camping sites: 14 tent-only picnic/camping sites
Maximum length: N/A
Facilities: Toilets, drinking water
Fees per night: None
Management: U.S. Army Corps of Engineers
Contact: (254) 694-3189
Finding the campground: From Hillsboro, take TX 22 west through the city of Whitney and across the Whitney Dam (approximately 24 miles). Soldiers Bluff will be the first right after crossing the dam.
About the campground: Soldiers Bluff Recreation Area is located on the west end of the Whitney Dam.

2.63 Lake Whitney–Lake Whitney State Park

Location: Whitney
Entrance fee: Small fee
Season: Open year-round, except during public hunts
Camping sites: 137 sites with water, electric, and/or sewer hookups
Maximum length: No length restrictions
Facilities: Restrooms with and without showers, dump station, picnic sites with and without shade shelters
Fees per night: $–$$
Management: Texas Parks & Wildlife Department
Contact: (254) 694-3793
Finding the campground: From Hillsboro, take TX 22 west 3 miles to Whitney and follow the signs to Lake Whitney State Park. The park is located 3 miles west of Whitney on FM 1244.
About the campground: This 995-acre park is on the east shore of Lake Whitney, west of Hillsboro in Hill County. Activities include hiking, mountain biking, picnicking, boating, fishing, swimming, scuba diving, waterskiing, nature study, and excellent birding. Amenities include an airstrip with a 2,000-foot paved runway (unlighted, unattended, left-hand pattern, call traffic on 122.9 MHz); a fish-cleaning facility; and a boat-launching ramp.

Belton Lake

	Campsites	Total Sites	Max RV Length	Hookups	Toilets	Showers	Drinking Water	Dump Station	Recreation	Fee
2.64 Cedar Ridge Park	TR	68	U	WE	F	X	X	X	SFBL	$$-$$$
2.65 Iron Bridge Park	T	5	N/A		NF				FBL	
2.66 Live Oak Ridge Park	TR	48	U	WE	F	X	X	X	FBL	$$-$$$
2.67 White Flint Park	TR	27	U	WE	F	X	X		SFBL	$$-$$$
2.68 Winkler Park	TR	15	35	W	F	X	X		SFBL	
2.69 McGregor Park	T	7	N/A		NF				FBL	
2.70 Owl Creek Park	T	10	N/A		NF				FBL	
2.71 Westcliff Park	TR	38	U	WE	F	X	X	X	SFBL	$$-$$$

Belton Lake is a U.S. Army Corps of Engineers reservoir, located on the Leon River in the Brazos River basin, 5 miles northwest of Belton. Fish present in the lake include largemouth bass, smallmouth bass, white bass, hybrid striped bass, catfish, and sunfish. The lake is especially popular among anglers for hybrid striped bass, and can also be a good largemouth lake at certain times of the year.

The main lake area is dominated by steep, rough limestone shoreline on the south end. Majestic tall bluffs and long rocky points are most common, though sand and mud flats can be found up the Leon River and Cowhouse arms. The north side of the lake has easier access, with a gentle sloping shoreline. There is a limited amount of standing timber, and the lake has little or no aquatic vegetation.

2.64 Belton Lake–Cedar Ridge Park

Location: Belton, on the east shore at midlake
Entrance fee: None
Season: Park open daily 6:00 a.m. to 10:00 p.m.
Camping sites: 68 sites with water and electric hookups
Maximum length: No length restrictions
Facilities: Restrooms with hot showers, dump station, camper service center with washers and dryers
Fees per night: $$-$$$

Management: U.S. Army Corps of Engineers

Contact: (254) 939-2461

Finding the campground: From Belton, travel 3 miles north on TX 317, turn left on TX 36 and watch for signs.

About the campground: Gate attendants reside within the park to serve visitors. Amenities include a two-lane boat ramp, fishing dock, swimming beach, and playgrounds. Pier 36 Marina (254-986-2466) is located at Cedar Ridge Park and has boat slips for rent, a snack bar, gas, and Jeff's Crab Shack restaurant.

2.65   Belton Lake–Iron Bridge Park

Location: Belton, uplake on the Leon River channel

Entrance fee: None

Season: Open year-round

Camping sites: 5 basic sites

Maximum length: Not suitable for RVs

Facilities: Vault toilets

Fees per night: None

Management: U.S. Army Corps of Engineers

Contact: (254) 939-2461

Finding the campground: From I-35 at Temple, go northwest 9 miles on TX 36. Cross the lake and watch for the Iron Bridge Park sign, where you turn right.

About the campground: A two-lane boat ramp is available.

2.66   Belton Lake–Live Oak Ridge Park

Location: Belton, downlake on the east shore

Entrance fee: None (entrance restricted to campers)

Season: Open year-round

Camping sites: 48 sites with 30- or 50-amp electric and water hookups

Maximum length: No length restrictions

Facilities: Restrooms with hot showers, dump station, camper service center with washers and dryers

Fees per night: $$–$$$

Management: U.S. Army Corps of Engineers

Contact: (254) 939-2461

Finding the campground: From I-35 in Belton, take FM 317 to Exit FM 439, travel west about 4 miles to the park.

About the campground: Live Oak Ridge is located on a ridge overlooking the lake and is well shaded with large oak trees. The boat launch ramp will handle all boat types. Gate attendants reside at the campground.

2.67   Belton Lake–White Flint Park

Location: Belton, uplake on the west shore
Entrance fee: None
Season: Open year-round
Camping sites: 13 tent/RV sites with water and electric hookups; 14 sites without hookups; 4 tent-only sites
Maximum length: No length restrictions
Facilities: Restrooms with hot showers
Fees per night: $$-$$$
Management: U.S. Army Corps of Engineers
Contact: (254) 939-2461
Finding the campground: From I-35 in Temple, take TX 36, west towards Gatesville (approx 10 miles). Just after Leon River Bridge, turn right on White Flint Park Road, and follow it to the park entrance.
About the campground: White Flint campground is located on the upper part of the lake, with plenty of shoreline access for fishing. A two-lane boat ramp (small launch fee), swimming beach, and playground are available.

2.68   Belton Lake–Winkler Park

Location: Belton, uplake on the west shore
Entrance fee: None
Season: Open year-round
Camping sites: 15 basic sites
Maximum length: 35 feet
Facilities: Restrooms with showers, drinking water
Fees per night: No fee
Management: U.S. Army Corps of Engineers
Contact: (254) 939-2461
Finding the campground: From I-35 in Temple, take TX 36, west towards Gatesville (approx 10 miles). Just after Leon River Bridge, turn right on White Flint Park Road, turn left on Winkler Park Road and follow it to the park entrance.
About the campground: The camping is semiprimitive at this isolated park. Winkler is a popular fishing camp, and most winter campers come to fish for near record-size flathead catfish, also called yellow cats. There is a camp host that stays in the park year-round to serve the campers. Swimming areas, with a good beach, are available at the north end of the park, and the launch ramp can handle all boat types.

2.69 Belton Lake–McGregor Park

Location: Belton
Entrance fee: None
Season: Open year-round
Camping sites: 7 picnic/camping sites
Maximum length: N/A
Facilities: Vault toilets
Fees per night: None
Management: U.S. Army Corps of Engineers
Contact: (254) 939-2461
Finding the campground: The campground is located off TX 36 and McGregor Park Road.
About the campground: This park has picnic/camping sites with excellent water access, but no water or electricity is available. It also has a one-lane boat ramp.

2.70 Belton Lake–Owl Creek Park

Location: Belton
Entrance fee: None
Season: Open year-round
Camping sites: 10 picnic/camping sites
Maximum length: N/A
Facilities: Vault toilets
Fees per night: None
Management: U.S. Army Corps of Engineers
Contact: (254) 939-2461
Finding the campground: From I-35 at Temple, go northwest on TX 36 about 18 miles. Cross the lake and watch for the turn to Owl Creek Park on the left.
About the campground: This park has excellent shade; however, the campsites are not close to the water. There is no water or electricity in this park, but it does have a two-lane boat ramp and toilet facilities.

2.71   Belton Lake–Westcliff Park

Location: Belton
Entrance fee: Day-use fee
Season: Park open daily 6:00 a.m. to 10:00 p.m.
Camping sites: 27 tent/RV sites with water and electric hookups; 11 primitive tent-only sites
Maximum length: No length restrictions
Facilities: Restrooms with hot showers, dump station, picnic tables, grills
Fees per night: $$–$$$
Management: U.S. Army Corps of Engineers
Contact: (254) 939-2461
Finding the campground: From TX 317 in Belton, go west on FM 439 about 6 miles. Pass the dam and watch for park signs.
About the campground: Most of the sites are located along the shoreline, close to the water. The park is staffed with gate attendants to assist visitors. A two-lane boat ramp, swimming beach, and playground are available.

Waco Lake

	Campsites	Total Sites	Max RV Length	Hookups	Toilets	Showers	Drinking Water	Dump Station	Recreation	Fee
2.72 Airport Park RA	TR	74	U	WES	F		X		FBL	$$-$$$
2.73 Midway Park RA	TR	38	U	WES	F		X		FBL	$$-$$$
2.74 Reynolds Creek Park RA	TR	57	U	WE	F		X	X	FBL	$$-$$$
2.75 Speegleville Park	TRS	32	U	WE	F		X	X	FBL	$$-$$$

Waco Lake has four campgrounds—Airport Park, Midway Park, Reynolds Creek Park, and Speegleville Park—located around it, offering various types of recreation such as boating, jet skiing, waterskiing, fishing, and swimming, along with birding areas with trails. Airport Park, on the north shore of the lake, also has a marina and restaurant.

Over fifty species of fish inhabit Waco Lake. The most common include large-mouth bass, white bass, crappie, channel catfish, blue catfish, and yellow catfish. The crappie fishing is hard to beat here, and fishing for largemouth bass, white bass, catfish, and sunfish is also good, especially in the spring. The main lake shoreline has lots of willow trees that hold fish year-round, except during low water levels. The North and South Bosque Rivers have an abundance of standing timber and laydowns.

2.72   Waco Lake–Airport Park Recreation Area

Location: Waco, on the north shore of the lake
Entrance fee: Small fee
Season: Park open daily 6:00 a.m. to 10:00 p.m.
Camping sites: 21 sites with sewer, water, and electric hookups; 38 sites with water and electric hookups; 15 primitive sites with water only
Maximum length: No length restrictions
Facilities: Flush toilets, drinking water, picnic areas
Fees per night: $$-$$$
Management: U.S. Army Corps of Engineers
Contact: (254) 756-5359
Finding the campground: Airport Park is located on the North Shore of the lake 1/4 mile west of the dam. From I-35 take Lake Shore Drive, exit west to Steinbeck Bend Road, right to Airport Road then turn right, go 2 miles. Park on the left.

About the campground: The campground includes a group shelter with eight sites, some with electric/water/sewer hookups, that is perfect for large groups. A two-lane boat ramp (small launch fee) is also available.

2.73 Waco Lake–Midway Park Recreation Area

Location: Midway Park is located on the east shore of the South Bosque River
Entrance fee: None
Season: Park open daily 6:00 a.m. to 10:00 p.m.
Camping sites: 11 sites with water, electric, and sewer hookups; 22 sites with water and electric hookups; 5 primitive tent sites
Maximum length: No length restrictions
Facilities: Flush toilets, drinking water, picnic areas
Fees per night: $$–$$$
Management: U.S. Army Corps of Engineers
Contact: (254) 756-5359
Finding the campground: From I-35, take TX 6 for about 5 miles, exit right at Midway Park exit, circle under bridge; park is 1/2 mile down service road.
About the campground: Midway Park is located on the east shore of the South Bosque River. A two-lane boat ramp (small launch fee) is available.

2.74 Waco Lake–Reynolds Creek Park Recreation Area

Location: Waco, on the west shore of the lake
Entrance fee: None
Season: Park open daily 6:00 a.m. to 10:00 p.m.
Camping sites: 51 sites with water and 30- or 50-amp electric hookups; 6 primitive tent sites
Maximum length: No length restrictions
Facilities: Flush toilets, dump station, drinking water, picnic areas
Fees per night: $$–$$$
Management: U.S. Army Corps of Engineers
Contact: (254) 756-5359
Finding the campground: From I-35, take TX 6 north for about 7 miles to Speegleville Road and exit right. About 1 mile down Speegleville Road you will come to a four-way stop; continue straight to the entrance of the park.
About the campground: Waco Lake offers several educational programs, one being the amphitheater programs presented during the summer at Reynolds Creek Park. From Memorial Day weekend through Labor Day weekend, a program is presented at the amphitheater each Saturday night, starting at sunset and ending at 10:00 p.m., on such topics as hunting, fishing, snakes, birds, lake history, water safety, and camping. The park also has a two-lane boat ramp (small launch fee).

2.75 Waco Lake–Speegleville Park

Location: Waco, on the west shore of the lake
Entrance fee: Small fee
Season: Park open daily 6:00 a.m. to 10:00 p.m.
Camping sites: 21 sites with water and electric hookups; 9 sites with electric only; 2 screened shelters
Maximum length: No length restrictions
Facilities: Flush toilets, dump station, drinking water, picnic areas
Fees per night: $$–$$$
Management: U.S. Army Corps of Engineers
Contact: (254) 756-5359
Finding the campground: From I-35, take TX 6 north toward Meridian for about 6 miles. After crossing the lake on the Twin Bridges, take the first exit and turn left on the access road. Continue past Twin Bridges Park about 0.25 mile until you reach Overflow Road. Once on Overflow Road, continue driving until you reach the park entrance.
About the campground: Reservations cannot be made for this campground. A four-lane boat ramp is available.

Prairies and Lakes 2

		Campsites	Total Sites	Max RV Length	Hookups	Toilets	Showers	Drinking Water	Dump Station	Recreation	Fee
2.76	Bastrop SP	TR	127	U	WESI	F	X	X		HFSBCJ	$$
2.77	Buescher SP	TR	57	U	WE	F	X	X	X	HFBC	$$
2.78	Fort Parker SP	TR	28	U	WE	F	X	X	X	HSFBLCJ	$-$$
2.79	Granger Lake—Taylor RA	TR	48	U	WE	F	X	X	X	FBL	$$
2.80	Granger Lake—Willis Creek RA	TR	27	U	WES	F	X	X	X	FBL	$$
2.81	Granger Lake—Wilson H. Fox RA	TR	58	U	WES	F	X	X	X	SFBL	$$
2.82	Lockhart SP	TR	20	U	WES	F	X	X		HSF	$$
2.83	Mother Neff SP	TR	24	U	WE	F	X	X		HF	$-$$
2.84	Palmetto SP	TR	38	U	WES	F	X	X	X	HSFBJ	$$

Granger Lake features three parks containing 133 class A campsites. For the angler, crappie is the most popular sport fish in this reservoir. Channel, flathead, and blue catfish are present in good numbers, and white bass provide a consistent fishery. A small number of largemouth bass are also present and provide a marginal fishery. Flooded willows, stumps, and laydowns dominate Granger. Generally speaking, it is a very shallow reservoir with turbid water. The best cover/structure is found in the old creek channels, main-lake humps and ridges, and up the San Gabriel River. In the main lake, submerged man-made brush piles consistently attract crappie.

Bastrop State Park is the site of the famous "Lost Pines," an isolated timbered region of loblolly pines and hardwoods. One of the more popular activities at the park is biking. Whether you are a beginner or an expert rider, you will find what you are looking for on the 12-mile scenic ride on Park Road 1C between Bastrop and Buescher State Parks.

Canoeing is popular at Fort Parker and Palmetto State Parks. At Fort Parker, the 3-mile canoe trip on the Navasota River begins at the Confederate Reunion Grounds and ends at Fort Parker. Fort Parker State Park offers canoe shuttle service when prearranged.

The San Marcos River runs through Palmetto State Park. Boaters can put in at Luling City Park and travel 14 miles to Palmetto, portaging around one dam along the way; or put in at Palmetto and take out at the Slayden bridge, 7.5 miles downriver. It is a two-day trip from Luling City Park to the Slayden bridge, staying overnight in Palmetto along the way.

2.76 Bastrop State Park

Location: Bastrop
Entrance fee: Small fee
Season: Open year-round
Camping sites: 50 primitive backpack sites (minimum 1-mile hike); 7 walk-in (60 yards) sites; 16 tent sites with water; 19 sites with water and electric hookups; 35 sites with electric, water, and sewer hookups
Maximum length: No length restrictions
Facilities: Restrooms with showers; walk-in sites have a picnic table, waist-high grill, fire ring, 15-by-15-foot tent pad, water in the area; tent sites in Deer Run area have a picnic table, waist-high grill, fire ring, 15-by-15-foot tent pad; sites with water and electric hookups in Copperas Creek Camp area have a picnic table, waist-high grill, fire ring, and 20/30-amp receptacles (all sites are back-in); sites with full hookups in Piney Hill Camp area (pull-through) and Copperas Creek Camp area (back-in) have a picnic table, waist-high grill, fire ring, and 20/30/50-amp receptacles.
Fees per night: $$
Management: Texas Parks & Wildlife Department
Contact: (512) 321-2101
Finding the campground: From Bastrop, take TX 21 east for 1 mile to the park entrance.
About the campground: Bastrop State Park covers 5,926 total acres and is approximately 30 miles southeast of Austin in Bastrop County. It is the site of the famous "Lost Pines," an isolated timbered region of loblolly pines and hardwoods. The park provides opportunities for backpacking, hiking, picnicking, canoeing (rentals available), golfing, and wildlife viewing, along with interpretive programs and a swimming pool. WiFi is available for park visitors to use.

2.77 Buescher State Park

Location: Smithville
Entrance fee: Small fee
Season: Open year-round
Camping sites: 32 sites with electric and water hookups; 25 sites with water only
Maximum length: No length restrictions
Facilities: Restrooms with and without showers, dump station
Fees per night: $$
Management: Texas Parks & Wildlife Department
Contact: (512) 237-2241
Finding the campground: From Smithville, take TX 71 north 2 miles to FM 153, then go north on FM 153 for 0.5 mile to Park Road 1 and the park entrance.
About the campground: Buescher State Park, a scenic area, encompasses nearly 1,017 acres just north of Smithville. Activities include nonmotorized boating (no ramp/small lake), fishing in a stocked lake, nature study, hiking on 7.5 miles of trails, and interpretive tours. The scenic, 12-mile-long, winding, and hilly paved road between Buescher and Bastrop State Parks is ideal for biking, but should only be used by experienced cyclists. A playground and group picnic pavilion are also available.

2.78 Fort Parker State Park

Location: Mexia
Entrance fee: Small fee
Season: Park open daily 8:00 a.m. to 10:00 p.m.
Camping sites: 25 sites with electric and water hookups; 3 hike-in (3 miles minimum) primitive camp-sites (cleared areas with a fire ring; bring your own water and pack out everything that you pack in)
Maximum length: No length restrictions
Facilities: Restrooms with and without showers, dump station
Fees per night: $-$$
Management: Texas Parks & Wildlife Department
Contact: (254) 562-5751
Finding the campground: The park is located 7 miles south of Mexia, or 6 miles north of Groes-beck, on TX 14; the entrance is on Park Road 28.
About the campground: Fort Parker State Park includes nearly 1,459 acres, 700 of which are lake. The park offers picnicking, swimming in an unsupervised area, fishing, bird-watching, hiking, biking, canoeing, and nature study. The canoe trip on the Navasota River from the Confederate Reunion Grounds to Fort Parker is 3 miles long. The park offers shuttle service for the canoes when prearranged (call 254-562-5751). Canoes are shuttled weekends only at 10:00 a.m., Mar through Nov. There is a four-hour minimum rental, and occupants need to supply their own trans-portation to and from the Confederate Reunion Grounds and Fort Parker State Park. A boat ramp and dock, a 1-mile multiuse trail (hiking and mountain biking), fishing pier, fish-cleaning facilities, playground, and baseball/softball field are also available.

2.79 Granger Lake–Taylor Recreation Area

Location: Granger
Entrance fee: Small fee
Season: Open year-round
Camping sites: 48 sites (back-in only) with electric and water hookups
Maximum length: No length restrictions
Facilities: Restrooms with showers, hot water, and flush toilets; dump station; water hydrants; covered picnic tables; stand-up cookers; fire rings; utility tables
Fees per night: $$
Management: U.S. Army Corps of Engineers
Contact: (512) 859-2668
Finding the campground: From I-35 in Round Rock, travel east on US 79 about 18 miles to Taylor, and take TX 95 north, approximately 7 miles, toward Granger. For Taylor Park turn right off TX 95 onto FM 1331 near Circleville and look for park signs on left.
About the campground: Known for great white bass and crappie fishing, Granger Lake also offers excellent hunting opportunities on the 10,000-plus-acre wildlife management area. Taylor Recre-ation Area offers a four-lane concrete boat ramp.

2.80   Granger Lake–Willis Creek Recreation Area

Location: Granger
Entrance fee: Small fee
Season: Open year-round
Camping sites: 27 sites (back-in only) with electric, water, and some sewer hookups
Maximum length: No length restrictions
Facilities: Restrooms with showers, hot water, and flush toilets; dump station; water hydrants; covered picnic tables; stand-up cookers; fire rings; utility tables
Fees per night: $$
Management: U.S. Army Corps of Engineers
Contact: (512) 859-2668
Finding the campground: From I-35 in Round Rock, travel east on US 79 to Taylor about 18 miles and take TX 95 north toward Granger approximately 7 miles. For Willis Creek Park, turn right onto CR 346 between the San Gabriel River and Granger.
About the campground: Granger Lake is known for great white bass and crappie fishing and also offers excellent hunting opportunities on the 10,000-plus-acre wildlife management area. A three-lane concrete boat ramp is available at this park.

2.81   Granger Lake–Wilson H. Fox Recreation Area

Location: Granger
Entrance fee: Small fee
Season: Open year-round
Camping sites: 58 sites with electric, water, and some sewer hookups
Maximum length: No length restrictions
Facilities: Restrooms with showers, hot water, and flush toilets; dump station; covered picnic tables; upright grills; fire rings
Fees per night: $$
Management: U.S. Army Corps of Engineers
Contact: (512) 859-2668
Finding the campground: From I-35 in Round Rock, travel east on US 79 approximately 18 to Taylor, and take TX 95 north approximately 7 miles toward Granger. For Wilson H. Fox Park, turn right off TX 95 onto FM 1331 near Circleville and look for park signs on left.
About the campground: Granger Lake is known for great white bass and crappie fishing. Two concrete ramps are available at the park, one six-lane and one two-lane, along with a swimming beach.

2.82   Lockhart State Park

Location: Lockhart
Entrance fee: Small fee
Season: Open year-round
Camping sites: 10 sites with electric and water hookups; 10 sites with electric, water, and sewer hookups
Maximum length: No length restrictions
Facilities: Restrooms with showers
Fees per night: $$
Management: Texas Parks & Wildlife Department
Contact: (512) 398-3479
Finding the campground: From Lockhart, go 1 mile south on US 183 to FM 20, then southwest on FM 20 for 2 miles to Park Road 10, then 1 mile south on Park Road 10.
About the campground: Lockhart State Park encompasses nearly 264 acres. Activities include picnicking, fishing, hiking on 1.5 miles of trails, nature study, a swimming pool, and a 9-hole golf course (fee charged).

2.83   Mother Neff State Park

Location: Moody
Entrance fee: Small fee
Season: Open year-round
Camping sites: 6 sites with electric and water hookups; 15 sites with water nearby; 3 hike-in (0.25 mile) primitive sites
Maximum length: No length restrictions
Facilities: Restrooms with and without showers, picnic tables, fire rings and/or grills
Fees per night: $-$$
Management: Texas Parks & Wildlife Department
Contact: (254) 853-2389
Finding the campground: From I-35, take exit 315 to TX 107 and head west about 8 miles to Moody. Continue 6 miles west on TX 107, then take TX 236 for 2 miles to the park.
About the campground: The main activities here are hiking, picnicking, fishing from the riverbank, and wildlife observation. A playground and an outdoor sports area are available. The primitive campsites are located on a prairie near a small pond. The other sites are heavily shaded, featuring large oak, pecan, and elm trees.

2.84   Palmetto State Park

Location: Gonzales
Entrance fee: Small fee
Season: Open year-round
Camping sites: 18 RV sites with 30/50-amp electric and water hookups (2 also have sewer); 20 tent sites with water (some premium)
Maximum length: No length restrictions
Facilities: Restrooms with showers and baby changing stations, dump station; RV sites (back-in) have a picnic table, fire ring, and grill; tent sites have a picnic table, fire ring, grill, and 16-by-16-foot (premium 24-by-24-foot) tent pad.
Fees per night: $$
Management: Texas Parks & Wildlife Department
Contact: (830) 672-3266
Finding the campground: From Gonzales, travel 10 miles northwest on US 183 to FM 1586, then west on FM 1586 for 2 miles to Ottine, then south on Park Road 11 for a couple miles.
About the campground: Palmetto State Park (270 acres) is named for the tropical dwarf palmetto plant found there and is located in Gonzales County, northwest of Gonzales and southeast of Luling. The park abuts the San Marcos River and also has a 4-acre oxbow lake. Activities include picnicking, hiking, fishing, bird-watching, nature study, swimming, tubing, and canoeing. Pedal boats and canoes are available for rental. Boaters can put in at Luling City Park and travel 14 miles down the San Marcos to Palmetto, portaging around one dam along the way; or put in at Palmetto and take out at the Slayden bridge, 7.5 miles downriver. It is a two-day trip from Luling City Park to the Slayden bridge, overnighting in Palmetto along the way.

The park, located on the Great Texas Coastal Birding Trail, has long been noted as a birding hot spot. Over 240 species of birds have been observed within the park's boundaries. Some of the birds most often spotted include the crested carcara, prothonotary warbler, and red-shouldered hawk.

Somerville Lake, Stephen F. Austin State Park, and Still House Hollow Lake

		Campsites	Total Sites	Max RV Length	Hookups	Toilets	Showers	Drinking Water	Dump Station	Recreation	Fee
2.85	Somerville Lake–Birch Creek	TR	176	U	WE	F	X	X	X	HFBLRC	$-$$
2.86	Somerville Lake–Overlook Park	TR	243	U	WE	F, NF		X	X	FBL	$$
2.87	Somerville Lake–Rocky Creek Park	TR	195	U	WE	F	X	X	X	HFBL	$$-$$$
2.88	Somerville Lake–Yegua Creek Park	TR	82	U	WE	F	X	X		HFBL	$$-$$$
2.89	Stephen F. Austin SP	TRS	80	U	WES	F	X	X		HF	$$-$$$
2.90	Still House Hollow Lake–Dana Peak Park	TR	25	U	WE	F	X	X	X	HSFBLRC	$-$$$
2.91	Still House Hollow Lake–Union Grove Park	TRS	37	U	WE	F	X	X	X	HSFBLC	$$-$$$

Somerville Lake covers 11,460 acres and is located in the south-central part of Burleson County and the north-central part of Washington County, with the upper reaches of the lake extending into Lee County. Fishing is allowed along the shoreline at all of the parks and at the spillway.

White bass anglers know this lake well as a high-quality fishery, especially during the spring spawning run. However, the lake also offers very good fishing for hybrid striped bass, channel catfish, and crappie. Largemouth bass are not quite as abundant, but good catches are reported, with fish up to 10 pounds. Both white bass and hybrid striped bass are taken in the creeks in late winter/early spring, usually beginning in mid-February. During summer and fall these two species are found in open water following schooling shad. The area off Welch Park is particularly good just before the spring spawning run.

Still House Hollow Lake is located 16 miles upstream of the confluence of the Lampasas and Leon Rivers that flow into the Little River. There are 58 miles of shoreline at the conservation pool. Recreation activities offered at Still House include camping, picnicking, fishing, boating, hiking, and wildlife watching. Hikers can enjoy 5 miles of trail in the Chalk Ridge Falls area, which is located below the Still House Lake Dam (open 8:00 am to sunset). A marina is located at Still House Hollow Lake Park off Simmons Road and can be contacted at (254) 939-5741.

2.85   Somerville Lake–Birch Creek

Location: Somerville
Entrance fee: Small fee
Season: Open year-round
Camping sites: 100 sites with 30- or 50-amp electric and water hookups; 50 hike-in (2.5–10 miles) primitive sites; 16 walk-in (20–100 yards) sites; 10 equestrian-only tent sites
Maximum length: No length restrictions
Facilities: Restrooms with and without showers, dump stations. Hookup sites have a picnic table and fire ring and/or grill; 4 are ADA compliant. Hike-in primitive sites are on the Trailway and can be accessed by foot/bike/horse; no potable water available, no open fires allowed, containerized fuel only. Walk-in sites have water in the area; 1 is ADA compliant. Equestrian-only tent sites have water nearby, a picnic table, tent pad, and combo fire ring/BBQ grill; 1 is ADA compliant. Gear must be carried from the parking lot to the equestrian sites (about 25 to 30 feet). Three 12-by-24-foot horse pens are in the area (first-come, first-served); each pen is divided into 2 12-by-12-foot sections (2 horses will fit in each section, 4 per pen). There are also 2 hitching areas at each site where horses could be tied, or you can tie them to your trailers.
Fees per night: $–$$
Management: Texas Parks & Wildlife Department
Contact: (409) 535-7763
Finding the campground: From Burton, take Spur 125 to FM 1697 and turn left. Travel on FM 1697 to FM 180 and turn right. Continue on FM 180 to the park.

About the campground: From fishing to horseback riding, Birch Creek offers a multitude of recreational opportunities. In the spring, fields full of wildflowers, including an abundance of bluebonnets, can be seen. Wildlife also abounds, including white-tailed deer, squirrels, rabbits, waterfowl, and songbirds. Amenities at the park include a fishing jetty, a fish-cleaning shelter, a family fishing pond, a convenience store adjacent to the park entrance, a sand and a grass volleyball court, a basketball court, a horseshoes pit, two double-lane boat ramps, a boat dock, and multiuse trails. The total trail mileage (including the Trailway) is 19, with 13 miles for backpacking and equestrian use and the entire 19 for day hiking, mountain biking, birding, and nature study.

2.86   Somerville Lake–Overlook Park

Location: Somerville
Entrance fee: N/A
Season: Open year-round
Camping sites: 193 sites with electricity and water; 50 sites with no electricity
Maximum length: No length restrictions
Facilities: Pit and flush toilets, dump station
Fees per night: $$
Management: Privately owned
Contact: Marina (979) 289-2321
Finding the campground: From Houston take US 290 west 70 miles to Brenham. Follow TX 36 north approximately 14 miles to FM 1948. Turn left. Cross railroad tracks. Turn right. Follow road for approximately 0.5 mile. Turn left into park complex. Follow road to end. Turn right.
About the campground: Amenities include a boat launch ramp, laundry facilities, a marina, and a convenience store.

2.87   Somerville Lake–Rocky Creek Park

Location: Burton
Entrance fee: None
Season: Open year-round
Camping sites: 34 sites with 20/30/50-amp electric and water hookups; 40 sites with 20/30-amp electric and water hookups; 75 basic sites with water available; 46 primitive sites with water nearby
Maximum length: No length restrictions
Facilities: Restrooms with showers, dump station
Fees per night: $$–$$$
Management: U.S. Army Corps of Engineers
Contact: (979) 596-1622
Finding the campground: From Brenham, follow TX 36 north approximately 14 miles to FM 1948. Turn left, follow FM 1948 about 5 miles, and turn right into the park complex.

About the campground: Rocky Creek is a large campground with lots of big trees, a playground, nature trail, and boat ramp (small launch fee).

2.88 Somerville Lake–Yegua Creek Park

Location: Burton
Entrance fee: None
Season: Open year-round
Camping sites: 47 sites with 20/30-amp electric and water hookups; 35 sites with water nearby
Maximum length: No length restrictions
Facilities: Restrooms with showers
Fees per night: $$-$$$
Management: U.S. Army Corps of Engineers
Contact: (979) 596-1622
Finding the campground: From Brenham, follow TX 36 north approximately 14 miles to FM 1948. Turn left, follow FM 1948 about 2.5 miles, and turn right into the park complex.
About the campground: The park has a playground, boat ramp (small launch fee), off-road-vehicle area, and nature trail.

2.89 Stephen F. Austin State Park

Location: San Felipe
Entrance fee: Small fee
Season: Open year-round
Camping sites: 38 sites with electric, water, and sewer hookups; 3 sites with electric and water hookups; 39 sites with water only
Maximum length: No length restrictions
Facilities: Restrooms with and without showers; laundry tubs; group screened dining hall for overnight use (includes grill; fire ring; 10 picnic tables; kitchen with refrigerator, cook stove, and hot and cold running water); group dining hall for day use (includes kitchen with cook stove, refrigerator, and sink; 10 tables; restrooms; and air-conditioning); group picnic pavilion
Fees per night: $$-$$$
Management: Texas Parks & Wildlife Department
Contact: (979) 885-3613
Finding the campground: From Houston, travel west 60 miles on I-10 to FM 1458, just before Sealy. Turn right (north) on FM 1458, then left on Park Road 38. The park is about 7 miles off I-10.
About the campground: Twelve acres of the park are set aside in honor of the area's past. Located on the Brazos River, adjoining the old ferry site and a part of the Commercio Plaza de San Felipe, this is the site of the township of San Felipe, the seat of government of the Anglo-American colonies in Texas. It was here Stephen F. Austin, the "Father of Texas," brought the first 297 families to colonize Texas under a contract with the Mexican government.

Activities at the park include picnicking, fishing, hiking, golf, and nature and historical tours. There is 5-mile hiking trail and a 0.25-mile nature/interpretive trail. The 18-hole golf course is operated by the Stephen F. Austin Golf Association (pro shop 979-885-2811; club 979-885-7203).

2.90 Still House Hollow Lake–Dana Peak Park

Location: Belton
Entrance fee: None
Season: Open year-round
Camping sites: 5 tent-only sites, 5 tent/trailers/RV sites, 2 pull-through RV sites, 3 double sites, and 2 mini group shelters, all with water and electric hookups; 8 tent-only primitive sites
Maximum length: No length restrictions
Facilities: Restroom with hot showers, dump station
Fees per night: $–$$$
Management: U.S. Army Corps of Engineers
Contact: (254) 939-2461
Finding the campground: From I-35 in Belton, take US 190 west to Simmons Road exit. Cross under the highway and turn west on FM 2410. Turn south on Comanche Gap Road and follow for 5 miles into the park.
About the campground: The Dana Peak Trail is located on Dana Peak Road before the main entrance to the park and is designed for hiking, biking, and equestrian use, with a corral and water trough for the horses. This is a free area that is open during daylight hours year-round. A fishing pier and four-lane concrete boat ramp are available for a small fee, along with a swimming beach.

2.91 Still House Hollow Lake–Union Grove Park

Location: Salado
Entrance fee: Small fee
Season: Open year-round
Camping sites: 24 tent/trailer/RV sites, 7 tent-only sites, 4 pull-through sites, and 2 double sites, all with water and electric hookups
Maximum length: No length restrictions
Facilities: Restroom with hot showers, dump station
Fees per night: $$–$$$
Management: U.S. Army Corps of Engineers
Contact: (254) 939-2461
Finding the campground: From I-35 in Salado, take FM 2484 exit. Travel west about 5 miles to Union Grove Park Road and then turn right.
About the campground: This park offers RV and tent camping, with water and electric hookups available at all sites. Fish present in Still House Lake include largemouth bass, smallmouth bass, white bass, catfish, and crappie. A fishing pier and four-lane concrete boat ramp are available for a small fee, along with a swimming beach.

Pineywoods

The Pineywoods travel region is bordered by Oklahoma and Arkansas on the north and Louisiana on the east. The landscape changes to an area of lush growth, low valleys surrounded by rolling hills, and plentiful water in the form of numerous lakes, rivers, and streams. Four national forests and national grasslands lie within the Pineywoods.

Marshall, Longview, and Tyler are three of the major towns in the northern half of Pineywoods. Opportunities for exploring the history of the region abound. Campers can visit the Starr Family State Historic Site in Marshall; nearby is the childhood home of Mrs. Lyndon B. Johnson and the Old City of Jefferson, famous as the commercial center of northeast Texas during the first half of the nineteenth century.

Caddo Indians once made the area around Atlanta their home. The Caddo settled the area peacefully as farmers, unlike their nomadic and warlike brothers, the Apache and Comanche found in west Texas. Excavations conducted by the Smithsonian Institute produced many graves and artifacts, and archaeologists found evidence of a house pattern with post molds still intact.

No matter where your travels in Texas may take you, the Pineywoods of east Texas is a great place to explore and camp. Well-equipped and maintained campgrounds exist as starting points for your explorations at several Texas state parks and national forests.

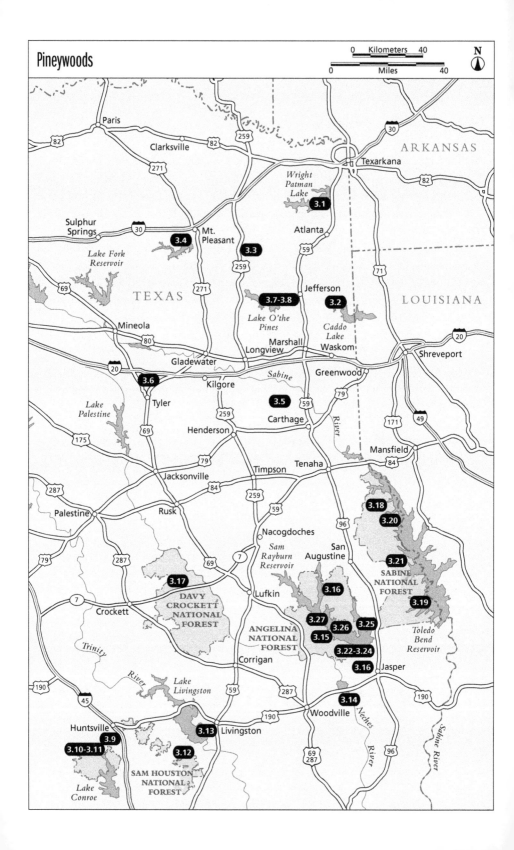

Pineywoods

0 Kilometers 40
0 Miles 40

N

Northern Pineywoods Region

		Campsites	Total Sites	Max RV Length	Hookups	Toilets	Showers	Drinking Water	Dump Station	Recreation	Fee
3.1	Atlanta SP	TR	66	40	WES	F	X	X	X	HSFBLCJ	$-$$
3.2	Caddo Lake SP	TR	54	U	WES	F	X	X	X	HSFBLJ	$-$$
3.3	Daingerfield SP	TR	44	U	WES	F	X	X	X	HSFBLJ	$-$$$
3.4	Lake Bob Sandlin SP	TRS	97	U	WE	F	X	X	X	HFSBLC	$-$$
3.5	Martin Creek Lake SP	TRS	91	U	WE	F	X	X	X	HFSBLC	$-$$
3.6	Tyler SP	TRS	149	U	WES	F	X	X	X	HBFBJCJ	$$-$$$
3.7	Lake of the Pines—Alley Creek Camp	TR	64	U	WEP	F	X	X	X	FBL	$$-$$$
3.8	Lake of the Pines—Buckhorn Creek	TR	53	U	WEP	F	X	X	X	FBL	$$-$$$

Explore enchanting Caddo Lake through a maze of quiet sloughs, bayous, and ponds lined with bald cypress trees draped in moss. The lake's headwaters begin in northeastern Texas, with the main body of the lake extending into Louisiana. Indian legend has it that the lake was formed by a giant flood, but scientists believe the lake formed when floodwaters blocked by massive logjams on the Red River backed up into the Cypress Bayou watershed, forming 28,810 acres of cypress swamp.

Guided lake tours on pontoon boats are available from Caddo Lake State Park and several other vendors around the lake; don't forget to bring your camera. Stately cypress trees, American lotuses, lily pads, waterfowl, alligators, turtles, frogs, snakes, raccoons, minks, nutrias, beavers, squirrels, armadillos, and white-tailed deer abound around the lake. If you are an angler, Caddo Lake contains more than seventy species of fish. It is especially good for crappie, largemouth bass, and white bass.

September through December is an especially good time to visit and camp at Martin Creek Lake State Park, located southeast of Longview. An annual perch-fishing contest is held for children ages 4 to 12 the first Saturday in September. Late October through the first two weeks of November is usually a particularly scenic time. Campers marvel at the colorful foliage displayed by the many varieties of hardwoods, interspersed with loblolly and short-leaf pine trees.

3.1 Atlanta State Park

Location: 11 miles northwest of Atlanta
Entrance fee: Day-use fee (over age 12)
Season: Open year-round
Camping sites: 44 sites with electric and water hookups; 17 sites with electric, water, and sewer hookups; 5 primitive sites
Maximum length: 40 feet

Facilities: Restrooms with and without showers, dump station; tent pad, picnic table, water, fire pit, and grill at each site; group picnic pavilion with tables under shelter and adjacent, with grill, electricity, water, and nearby restrooms

Fees per night: $–$$

Management: Texas Parks & Wildlife Department

Contact: (903) 796-6476

Finding the campground: From Atlanta, take US 59 approximately 11 miles north to FM 96 and go west 9 miles to FM 1154, then north 2 miles to the Park Road 42 entrance (FM 1154 dead-ends at the park).

About the campground: Atlanta State Park is 1,475 acres on Lake Wright Patman. Caddo Indians, the most culturally advanced tribe in Texas, once made this area their home. Contrasting seasonal colors of the terrain, the lake, sunsets, and pine forest are breathtaking. The park offers a playground with swings and slides, sand volleyball courts, a basketball court, horseshoes pits, 3.8 miles of hiking trails, 1.2 miles of interpretive trails, an amphitheater, a shelter, and canoe rentals. Swimming is available at a designated sandy beach area on popular Wright Patman Lake. Crappie, largemouth bass, white bass, several species of sunfish, channel catfish, blue catfish, and flathead catfish are present in good numbers in the lake. Concrete boat-launching ramps and covered fish-cleaning areas are available. Bicycling is popular along the hilly park and area roads.

3.2　Caddo Lake State Park

Location: 15 miles northeast of Marshall

Entrance fee: Day-use fee (over age 12)

Season: Open year-round

Camping sites: 54 sites with water, electric, and/or sewer hookups

Maximum length: No length restrictions

Facilities: Restrooms with and without showers, dump station; 2-, 4-, and 6-person cabins ($$$)

Fee per night: $–$$

Management: Texas Parks & Wildlife Department

Contact: (903) 679-3351

Finding the campground: From Karnack, take TX 43 north 1 mile to FM 2198 and go east 0.5 mile to Park Road 2.

About the campground: Thick bald cypresses and a tangle of aquatic plants thrive in the waters at Caddo Lake State Park. Activities include hiking, swimming, picnicking, nature study, fishing, and boating (ramp available). There are canoe and johnboat with motor rentals (outside the park about 6 miles away) and pontoon boat tours daily except Wednesday.

3.3 Daingerfield State Park

Location: East of Daingerfield
Entrance fee: Day-use fee (over age 12)
Season: Open year-round
Camping sites: 44 sites with water, electric, and/or sewer hookups
Maximum length: No length restrictions
Facilities: Restrooms with and without showers, dump station, overflow camping area, group lodge ($$$), 4- and 6-person cabins with heating/air-conditioning and kitchen facilities ($$$)
Fee per night: $-$$$
Management: Texas Parks & Wildlife Department
Contact: (903) 645-2921
Finding the campground: From Mt. Pleasant, take TX 49 southwest 22 miles to Daingerfield State Park (about 22 miles from I-30).
About the campground: Springtime brings breathtaking bouquets throughout the park's rolling hills when dogwoods, redbuds, and wisteria vines burst into bloom. Although northeast Texas is known for pines, every fall the park is a delight as sweetgum, oak, and maple trees produce dazzling shades of red and gold, offering a stark contrast to the evergreens. The park offers picnicking, boating (5-mph speed limit), fishing, swimming in an unsupervised area, hiking on 2.5 miles of trails, nature study, a playground with slides and swings, and picnic sites, including a group picnic area with tables (not covered). A seasonal concession (Mar–Oct) rents pedal boats and canoes, and a launching ramp, boat dock, fishing pier, and fish-cleaning facility are also available.

3.4 Lake Bob Sandlin State Park

Location: Approximately 12 miles southwest of Mt. Pleasant
Entrance fee: Day-use fee (over age 12)
Season: Open year-round
Camping sites: 75 campsites with water and electricity hookups; 2 primitive campsites with no improvements; 12 screened shelters; and 8 shelters with amenities
Maximum length: No length restrictions
Facilities: Restrooms with showers, screened shelters, limited-use cabins ($$$)
Fee per night: $-$$
Management: Texas Parks & Wildlife Department
Contact: (903) 572-5531
Finding the campground: From Mt. Vernon, take TX 37 south for 0.8 mile. Turn left on TX 21 and go 11.2 miles to the park entrance.
About the campground: Lake Bob Sandlin State Park is a 640-acre park located on the heavily wooded shoreline of the north side of 9,400-acre Lake Bob Sandlin. Varieties of oak, hickory, pine,

dogwood, redbud, and maple produce spectacular fall color. Activities include picnicking, in-line skating, hiking, mountain biking, swimming, and fishing for largemouth bass, catfish, and crappie. The park features 5 miles of hiking and mountain biking trails with eight footbridges, a playground, lighted fishing pier, fish-cleaning facility, two-lane boat ramp, and Texas State Park Store. Eagles can be spotted during winter months, and a variety of birds and wildlife can be viewed year-round. Interpretive tours and nature walks are given on some weekends and by request.

3.5   Martin Creek Lake State Park

Location: 20 miles southeast of Longview
Entrance fee: Day-use fee (over age 12)
Season: Open year-round
Camping sites: 12 primitive tent only campsites; 36 campsites with electric and water hookups; 15 premium (lake front access) campsites with electric and water hookups; 7 campsites with (50 amp) electric and water hookups; 19 screened shelters; and 2 shelters with amenities
Maximum length: No length restrictions
Facilities: Restrooms with showers, screened shelters, 2 cabins ($$$)
Fee per night: $-$$
Management: Texas Parks & Wildlife Department
Contact: (903) 836-4336
Finding the campground: From Tatum, take TX 43 southwest 3.5 miles to CR 2183 and continue south to the park.
About the campground: Martin Creek Lake State Park, consisting of 287 acres, is located on 5,000-acre Martin Creek Lake. People have inhabited the park area and the land surrounding it since 200 BC. Until the eighteenth century, Caddo Indians and Spanish explorers lived in and traveled through this area. Later the Choctaw, Cherokee, and Kickapoo Indians migrated here in response to the increasing influx of Anglo-Americans. Traces of the old roadbed of Trammel's Trace can still be seen near the fishing pier.

In 1833 Daniel Martin, for whom the park is named, settled with his family near the creek, called Hogan's Bayou at the time. He and his neighbors eventually built a small fort and then a town called Harmony Hill, which reached its heyday after the Civil War. It was deserted by 1900 and struck by a tornado in 1906. Traces of the old roads that brought prosperity to Harmony Hill can still be seen in the park and are part of the hiking trail.

Activities at the park include excellent year-round fishing, wildlife observation, picnicking, boating, waterskiing, unsupervised lake swimming, and interpretive programs on Saturdays. An annual perch-fishing contest is held for children ages 4 to 12 on the first Saturday in September. The park has a four-lane concrete boat ramp, lighted fishing pier, playground, 1.5-mile hiking trail, and 6-mile mountain biking trail. One of the primitive camping areas is located on an island accessed via a wooden bridge.

3.6   Tyler State Park

Location: 2 miles north of I-20
Entrance fee: Day-use fee (over age 12)
Season: Open year-round
Camping sites: 37 tent campsites with water; 20 campsites with electric and water hook-ups; 57 campsites with electric, water and sewer hook-ups; 29 screened shelters; and 6 shelters with amenities
Maximum length: No length restrictions
Facilities: Restrooms with and without showers, dump stations, trailer rally area (30 water and electric sites with a group picnic pavilion), group dining hall
Fee per night: $$-$$$
Management: Texas Parks & Wildlife Department
Contact: (903) 597-5338
Finding the campground: Tyler State Park is located 2 miles north of I-20 on FM 14 north of Tyler on Park Road 16.
About the campground: Activities at Tyler State Park include picnicking, boating (motors allowed; 5-mph speed limit), fishing, lake swimming, hiking, mountain biking, birding, and nature study. The park features an amphitheater on the lake shore; a seasonal grocery store that sells souvenirs and fishing supplies and rents canoes, paddleboats, kayaks, and fishing boats; a concrete launching ramp with a courtesy dock; a 2.5-mile hiking trail; a 13-mile mountain biking trail; and a 0.75-mile nature trail.

3.7   Lake of the Pines–Alley Creek Camp

Location: Approximately 16 miles from southeast of Jefferson
Entrance fee: None
Season: Open Mar through Sept
Camping sites: 49 RV campsites with electric and water hookups; 15 campsites designated for tent camping only.
Maximum length: No length restrictions
Facilities: Restrooms with hot showers and flush toilets (including a wheelchair accessible one), dump station, pay telephones; RV sites have a hard-surface pad (some available with tent pads), picnic table, fire ring, and lantern holder; tent sites have a picnic table, lantern holder, fire ring, and water hydrants nearby
Fee per night: $$-$$$
Management: U.S. Army Corps of Engineers
Contact: Park information (903) 665-2336; project office (903) 755-2637
Finding the campground: From Jefferson, travel 4 miles southeast on TX 49 to FM 729. Turn left and travel 12 miles west to the park entrance on the left.

About the campground: Alley Creek Campground is a highly developed multiuse park located on the north shore of Lake of the Pines, just off FM 729. In addition to overnight camping, the park provides a day-use area with six individual picnic sites. A ramp is available for launching boats for small fee.

3.8 Lake of the Pines–Buckhorn Creek

Location: Approximately 10 miles southeast of Jefferson
Entrance fee: None
Season: Open Mar through Sept
Camping sites: 38 RV sites with electric and water hookups; 15 tent-only sites
Maximum length: No length restrictions
Facilities: Restrooms with hot showers and flush toilets (one wheelchair accessible), dump station, pay telephones
Fee per night: $$–$$$
Management: U.S. Army Corps of Engineers
Contact: Park information (903) 665-2336; project office (903) 655-8261
Finding the campground: From Jefferson, travel 4 miles northwest on TX 49 to FM 729. Turn left and travel 3.5 miles west to FM 726, then turn left again and go 2.4 miles south to the park entrance on the right.
About the campground: Lake of the Pines provides excellent fishing, with catfish and bream the easiest to catch. The campground is located near the dam and has a great view of the lake.

Southern Pineywoods Region

	Campsites	Total Sites	Max RV Length	Hookups	Toilets	Showers	Drinking Water	Dump Station	Recreation	Fee
3.9 Huntsville SP	TRS	182	U	WE	F	X	X	X	HSFBLCJ	$$-$$$
3.10 Sam Houston NF—Stubblefield Lake Campground	TR	30	20	W	F	X	X		HF	$$
3.11 Sam Houston NF—Cagle RA	TR	47	U	WES	F	X	X		HFLB	$$$
3.12 Sam Houston NF—Double Lake RA	TR	65	U	WES	F	X	X		HSFBL	$$$
3.13 Lake Livingston SP	TRS	171	U	WES	F	X	X	X	HSFBLRC	$$-$$$
3.14 Angelina NF—Sandy Creek	T	15	N/A		NF				FBL	$-$$
3.15 Angelina NF—Caney Creek	T	123			NF	X	X	X	FBL	
3.16 Townsend Park	TR	19	U	W	NF			X	BL	$
3.17 Davy Crockett NF—Ratcliff Lake	TR	77	35	WE	F	X	X	X	HSFBLCJ	$$
3.18 Sabine NF—Boles Field	TR	20	U	WE	F	X	X		H	$
3.19 Sabine NF—Lakeview Campground	TR	10	U	W	NF		X		HF	$
3.20 Sabine NF—Ragtown RA	TR	25	U	W	F	X	X	X	HSFBL	$
3.21 Sabine NF—Red Hills Lake RA	TR	43	U	WE	F	X	X	X	SFBLJ	$-$$

This area contains numerous campsites lying within the boundaries of Huntsville and Lake Livingston State Parks, Townsend Park, and Sam Houston, Angelina, Davy Crockett, and Sabine National Forests. They are available for a multitude of recreation-oriented activities such as fishing, camping, hiking, photography, berry picking, bird-watching, picnicking, and general sightseeing.

Sam Houston National Forest hosts several campgrounds, including Stubblefield Lake Campground, Cagle Recreation Area, and Double Lake Recreation Area. Stubblefield Lake Campground is a fully developed area located on the south shore of the oxbow Stubblefield Lake. The Lone Star Hiking Trail, over 100 miles long, transects the campground. Fishing is popular on the nearby San Jacinto River bridge, Stubblefield Lake, and Lake Conroe. Cagle Recreation Area, located on Lake Conroe, has two camping loops surrounded by a 2-mile hiking trail. The southernmost mile of the trail is paved, for a less-primitive hiking experience.

Davy Crockett National Forest's Ratcliff Lake Recreation Area, built in 1936 by the Civilian Conservation Corps, surrounds a 45-acre lake. The lake was once a log pond and source of water for the Central Coal and Coke Company Sawmill, which logged the area from 1902 to 1920. The area offers visitors camping, picnicking, a swimming beach and bathhouse, boating, fishing, a concession stand, an amphitheater, and an interpretive trail in a beautiful forest setting that has been featured in regional magazines.

The 20-mile-long Four C National Recreation Trail begins at Ratcliff Lake and winds through a diverse forest of towering pines, bottomland hardwoods, boggy sloughs, and upland forests. Midway down the trail is the Walnut Creek campsite, with five tent pads, a shelter, and a pit toilet. Another campsite farther north on the trail has two tent pads. Neches Bluff Overlook, located at the north end of the trail, offers a panoramic view of pine/hardwood forests in the Neches River bottomlands along with picnic and primitive camping facilities.

Huntsville and Lake Livingston State Parks offer campsites compatible with the biggest of RVs to the smallest tent camper, including waterfront sites. Lake Raven, located within Huntsville State Park, offers excellent largemouth bass fishing. Raven is one of several lakes within the state whose bass population is being studied by Texas Parks & Wildlife fishery biologists in the hope of raising the next world-record bass.

Lake Livingston State Park, located on the shores of Lake Livingston, offers pier and bank fishing. Livingston is noted for its excellent white bass and catfish fishing. White bass are most readily caught in early spring in the many creeks that feed into the lake. Channel and blue catfish can be caught most any time of year on a variety of organic and live baits over the main river channel and in off-channel tributaries and creeks. Day-use horseback riding is now available here. Visitors must use the horses provided by Lake Livingston stables and are not allowed to bring their own.

3.9   Hunstville State Park

Location: 6 miles southwest of Huntsville
Entrance fee: Day-use fee (over age 12)
Season: Open year-round
Camping sites: 58 sites with electric and water hookups; 94 sites with water (some ADA accessible); 30 screened shelters
Length Maximum: No size restrictions
Facilities: Restrooms with and without showers; bathhouse; dump station; screened group picnic pavilion (capacity 75); group recreation hall (capacity 200); picnic table, fire ring, and BBQ grill at sites with hookups; overflow camping area ($)
Fees per night: $$–$$$
Management: Texas Parks & Wildlife Department
Contact: (936) 295-5644
Finding the campground: The park is 6 miles southwest of Huntsville off I-45 on Park Road 40.
About the campground: This heavily-wooded park adjoins the Sam Houston National Forest and encloses 210-acre Lake Raven. The lake is fed by three major creeks and offers fishing for crappie, perch, catfish, and bass. The woodlands are dominated by loblolly and shortleaf pines typical of the East Texas Pine Belt, providing attractive camping and picnic areas. Hiking trails have been constructed so that wildlife can be observed in a natural setting. White-tailed deer, raccoons, opossums, armadillos, fox squirrels, and migratory waterfowl are just a few of the creatures that may be discovered in their natural environment. Occasionally, alligators may be seen in the lake.

The park features a Texas State Park Store; fishing piers; fish-cleaning tables; boat rentals (seasonal, including paddleboats, canoes, and flat-bottoms without motors); a boat-launching ramp; a boat dock; a playground; a 0.75-mile interpretive nature trail; and 19 miles of hiking and biking trails. Waterskiing is prohibited due to the lake's size. Boat motor size is unrestricted; speed is limited to idle.

3.10   Sam Houston National Forest– Stubblefield Lake Campground

Location: North of Conroe
Entrance fee: Small fee
Season: Open year-round, except during deer firearms season, when camping is restricted to designated hunter camps
Camping sites: 30 basic sites
Maximum length: 20 feet
Facilities: Restrooms with flush toilets and hot showers; picnic table, fire ring, lantern post, and tent pad at each site
Fees per night: $$
Management: Sam Houston National Forest

Contact: (936) 344-6205 or (888) 361-6908

Finding the campground: Going north on I-45 from New Waverly, take FM 1375 west for 10.2 miles to Stubblefield Lake Road sign (FR 215). Turn right onto FR 215 and go 2.9 miles to the campground.

About the campground: This campground is located on the south shore of Stubblefield Lake, an oxbow lake on the upper reaches of Lake Conroe. The vegetation in the campground consists primarily of southern pines, oaks, gums, and dogwoods. It is a fairly open campground; however, there is thick vegetation between campsites, providing a private atmosphere. The Lone Star Hiking Trail transects the campground, and the Stubblefield Interpretive Trail is located directly to the north. Fishing is popular on the nearby San Jacinto River bridge, Stubblefield Lake, and Lake Conroe.

3.11 Sam Houston National Forest– Cagle Recreation Area

Location: Approximately 5 miles west of New Waverly

Entrance fee: Small fee

Season: Open year-round, except during deer firearms season, when camping is restricted to designated hunter camps

Camping sites: 47 sites with water, electric, and sewer hookups

Maximum length: No length restrictions

Facilities: Restrooms with flush toilets, sinks, and hot showers; tent pad, lantern post, and fire ring at each site

Fees per night: $$$

Management: Sam Houston National Forest

Contact: (936) 344-6205 or (888) 361-6908

Finding the campground: From I-45, take exit 102 or 103 to FM 1375 and go west approximately 5 miles. Turn left at the large Cagle Recreation Area sign.

About the campground: Cagle Recreation Area is located on the shore of Lake Conroe, with its great fishing and water sports. There is a boat ramp, hiking trails, and two camping loops, Sweet Gum and Sycamore, both of which have sites overlooking Lake Conroe. Some sites must be reserved (go to www.recreation.gov), and some are first-come, first-served. A 2-mile hiking trail surrounds the camping loops. The southernmost mile of the trail is paved for those wishing a less-primitive hiking experience.

3.12 Sam Houston National Forest– Double Lake Recreation Area

Location: Approximately 17 miles north of Cleveland

Entrance fee: Small fee

Season: Open year-round, except during deer firearms season, when camping is restricted to designated hunter camps
Camping sites: 65 sites with water, electric, and some sewer hookups, 37 of which are ADA accessible
Maximum length: No length restrictions
Facilities: Flush toilets, showers
Fees per night: $$$
Management: Sam Houston National Forest
Contact: (936) 344-6205 or (888) 361-6908
Finding the campground: From Coldspring, take TX 150 west 1.5 miles to Double Lake sign (FM 2025). Turn left onto FR 2025 and go 0.4 mile to Double Lake Recreation Area sign (FR 210). Turn left onto FR 210 and go 0.6 mile to campground.
About the campground: Double Lake offers a little of everything, including fishing, picnicking, and hiking. Sam Houston National Forest surrounds the area. Double Lake is stocked with bass, bream, and catfish. Anglers can fish from one of three piers or can take advantage of a limited-access boat ramp with parking nearby for trailers. Only boats with small electric trolling motors are allowed on the 23-acre lake. Swimmers enjoy relaxing on a sandy beach after taking a cool plunge, while hikers partake of the 5-mile trail leading to the Big Creek Scenic Area. For a longer trek, there's nearby access to the Lone Star Hiking Trail.

3.13   Lake Livingston State Park

Location: 1 mile southwest of Livingston
Entrance fee: Day-use fee (over age 12)
Season: Open year-round
Camping sites: 56 sites with sewer, electric, and water hookups; 69 sites with electric and water hookups; 26 sites with water hookups; 10 premium (water view) sites with sewer, electric, and water hookups; 10 screened shelters (some ADA accessible)
Maximum length: No length restrictions
Facilities: Restrooms with and without showers, dump stations
Fees per night: $$-$$$
Management: Texas Parks & Wildlife Department
Contact: (936) 365-2201
Finding the campground: From Livingston, take US 59 south 1 mile to FM 1988. Go 4 miles west on FM 1988, then 0.5 mile north on FM 3126 to Park Road 65.
About the campground: The park offers picnicking, a swimming pool (Memorial Day to Labor Day), mountain biking, hiking, nature study, fishing (crappie, perch, catfish, and bass), and boating. Day-use equestrian is also now available. Visitors must use the horses provided by Lake Livingston stables and are not allowed to bring their own. There are 6.9 miles of multiuse trails available—along with boat ramps and a seasonal (Mar–Oct) park store and marina that offers bait, gas, and dock facilities. Several playgrounds are scattered throughout the park.

3.14   Angelina National Forest–Sandy Creek

Location: Approximately 13 miles east of Woodville
Entrance fee: None
Season: Open year-round
Camping sites: 15 basic campsites with no hookups; tables and grills available.
Maximum length: N/A – no RV sites
Facilities: Vault toilets
Fees per night: $-$$
Management: U.S. Army Corps of Engineers
Contact: (409) 384-6166 or (409) 429-3491
Finding the campground: From Zavalla, take TX 63 east for 14.8 miles to Sandy Creek Recreational Area sign. Turn left at sign and go 2.6 miles to campground.
About the campground: Sandy Creek is located on the southeast side of B. A. Steinhagen Lake, between the towns of Woodville and Jasper. The area provides an ideal setting to fish, camp, and boat.

3.15   Angelina National Forest–Caney Creek

Location: Zavalla
Entrance fee: Small fee
Season: Open year-round
Camping sites: 123 primitive campsites in the Caney Creek Recreation Area (no water, sewer or electricity hookups available at this area)
Maximum length: N/A
Facilities: None
Fees per night: Currently none (Call before planning your camping trip to this park.)
Management: USDA Forest Service
Contact: (936) 897-1068
Finding the campground: From Zavalla, take TX 63 east 6 miles. Turn left on FM 2743 for 6 miles, then left (northeast) on FR 336 for 1 mile.
About the campground: Caney Creek is a popular location for those who enjoy fishing the waters of Sam Rayburn Reservoir. The boat ramp provides access to the lake throughout the year.

3.16   Townsend Park

Location: Approximately 5 miles west of Broaddus
Entrance fee: No fee
Season: Open year-round
Camping sites: 19 basic sites
Maximum length: No length restrictions

Facilities: Portable toilet, picnic table and fire grill at each site, dump station available at nearby Jackson Hill Park for a small fee; no drinking water
Fees per night: $
Management: San Augustine County
Contact: (936) 275-2762
Finding the campground: From Broaddus, follow TX 147 north for 1 mile and turn left (west) on FM 1277. Follow FM 1277 for 3.5 miles, then turn left (west) on FM 2923 for 1.5 miles to entrance.
About the campground: Townsend Park, located on Sam Rayburn Reservoir, was completed in 1966 and provides visitors with a rustic camping experience in a tranquil setting. The boat ramp provides access to the lake most of the year. A group picnic shelter is located on the grounds, and it accommodates up to 50 people. In consideration of other visitors, no off-road vehicles may be ridden in the campground.

3.17 Davy Crockett National Forest–Ratcliff Lake

Location: 15 miles east of Crockett
Entrance fee: Small fee
Season: Open year-round
Camping sites: 51 basic sites; 26 sites with 20- or 30-amp electric hookups
Maximum length: 35 feet
Facilities: Restrooms with flush toilets and cold-water showers, dump station
Fees per night: $$
Management: U.S. Army Corps of Engineers
Contact: (936) 655-2299
Finding the campground: From Crockett, take TX 7 east 15 miles. The recreation area is on the left between Ratcliff and Kennard.
About the campground: The recreation area has hardwoods and pines, and the campground surrounds a small, 45-acre lake. Activities and amenities include hiking, swimming, biking, bird-watching, a boat ramp, canoe rentals, a fishing pier, and playgrounds.

3.18 Sabine National Forest–Boles Field

Location: About 8 miles east of Shelbyville
Entrance fee: None
Season: Open year-round
Camping sites: 20 sites with electric hookups
Maximum length: No length restrictions
Facilities: Restrooms with hot showers, drinking water
Fees per night: $
Management: USDA Forest Service
Contact: (409) 787-3870

Finding the campground: Follow TX 87 south from Center for 4 miles; turn left (east) on FM 2694 for 8 miles to entrance.

About the campground: A covered shelter and amphitheater are available for group reservation. Reservations for the shelter should be made early, as the area is popular with many groups. Visitors can hike to the nearby spring.

3.19 Sabine National Forest–Lakeview Campground

Location: About 16 miles south of Pineland
Entrance fee: Small fee
Season: Open Mar 1 through Oct 15
Camping sites: 10 basic sites
Maximum length: No length restrictions
Facilities: Vault toilets
Fees per night: $
Management: Sabine River Authority
Contact: (409) 565-2273
Finding the campground: From Pineland, take FM 2426 east 10 miles, then turn right (south) on TX 87 for 3 miles. Turn left (east) on FM 2928 for 3.5 miles to the end of the paved road; follow signs to Lakeview, approximately 4 miles.

About the campground: Lakeview Campground is located on 185,000-acre Toledo Bend Reservoir and is maintained and operated by the Sabine River Authority of Texas. The campground offers fishing and picnicking and is situated at the Lakeview trailhead for the Trail Between the Lakes, a 28-mile hiking trail that runs from Sam Rayburn Reservoir to Toledo Bend Reservoir. The trail is maintained with the help of the Golden Triangle Sierra Club.

3.20 Sabine National Forest– Ragtown Recreation Area

Location: Toledo Bend Reservoir
Entrance fee: Day-use fee
Season: Open year-round
Camping sites: 12 double-family camping units (large enough for 2 families); 13 single-family camping units (large enough for 1 family)
Maximum length: No length restrictions
Facilities: Restrooms with hot showers, dump station, drinking water
Fees per night: $
Management: USDA Forest Service
Contact: (409) 787-3870

Finding the campground: Follow TX 87 east from Center for 11 miles; turn left (east) on FM 139 for 6 miles; bear right onto FM 3184 and follow 4 miles to entrance.

About the campground: Ragtown offers something for everyone—camping, hiking, fishing, bird-watching, and viewing nature at its best! The recreation area is located along the Texas shoreline of Toledo Bend Lake, one of the South's largest reservoirs. The campground is nestled high on a bluff that faces east; the panoramic view of the lake makes sunrises spectacular. Ragtown Recreation Area was developed in a remote region of the Sabine National Forest, and is about 10 miles from a grocery store or gasoline station. Because of its remoteness, the campground offers the visitor an uncrowded camping experience. The campground is seldom filled to capacity, and usually has only a few visitors per week.

Mother Nature's Trail loops around the campground for approximately 1 mile. The trail winds through woodlands of magnificent oak and beech trees, with a few scattered southern pines creating a diverse landscape. The trail then stretches along the shoreline of Toledo Bend Reservoir. And if you love fishing, Toledo Bend fishing is fabulous! The lake abounds with largemouth bass, white perch, white bass, stripers, bream, and a variety of catfish. The area between the boat ramp (small fee for non-campers) and campsite #1 is not developed as a swimming area, but is open and conducive to swimming.

3.21 Sabine National Forest– Red Hills Lake Recreation Area

Location: Toledo Bend Reservoir
Entrance fee: Small fee
Season: Open year-round
Camping sites: 28 double family camping units (large enough for 2 families) and 15 single-family picnicking units (large enough for 1 family), both with and without electric hookups
Maximum length: No length restriction
Facilities: Restrooms with flush toilets and cold showers, dump station, drinking water; typical family camping unit consists of a table, fireplace, tent base, parking spur, and lantern post
Fees per night: $–$$
Management: USDA Forest Service
Contact: (409) 787-3870
Finding the campground: From the junction of TX 87 and TX 21 (Milam side of Pendleton Bridge, about the center of the lake), take TX 87 north approximately 3 miles to the sign on the east (right) side of road.
About the campground: Red Hills Lake Recreation Area is in the Yellowpine Ranger District of the Sabine National Forest. The picturesque 19-acre lake and the 17 surrounding acres provide a gentle outdoor experience for today's visitors. Amenities include a swimming beach, bathhouse, and small-boat launch. Bass, bream, and catfish have been stocked in Red Hills Lake, and fishing is permitted (except in the swim site) under applicable state laws. Rowboats and boats powered by electric motors are allowed on the lake.

Sam Rayburn Reservoir

		Campsites	Total Sites	Max RV Length	Hookups	Toilets	Showers	Drinking Water	Dump Station	Recreation	Fee
3.22	Ebenezer Park	TR	30		WE	F	X	X	X	SR	$$
3.23	Twin Dikes Park	TRS	46	U	WES	F	X	X	X	FBL	$$-$$$
3.24	Mill Creek Park	TR	110	U	WEP	F	X	X	X	SFBL	$$
3.25	San Augustine Park	TR	100	U	WE	F	X	X	X	SFBL	$$
3.26	Rayburn Park	TR	46	U	WE	F, NF	X	X	X	FBL	$$
3.27	Hanks Creek Park	TR	44	U	WEP	F, NF	X	X	X	SFBL	$$

Sam Rayburn Reservoir, located north of Jasper, is the largest lake wholly located within the state of Texas. The U.S. Army Corps of Engineers manages six developed campgrounds (Ebenezer, Twin Dikes, Mill Creek, San Augustine, Rayburn, and Hanks Creek) and four access points (boat ramp and parking at Monterey, Marion Ferry, Etoile, and Ralph McAlister), and leases commercial concessions at the Sam Rayburn Marina and Resort, Powell Park Marina, Jackson Hill Marina, and Shirley Creek Marina.

Excellent year-round fisheries exist for largemouth bass, crappie, and catfish. Anglers are most successful at catching largemouth bass during the fall, winter, and spring months, when, due to cooler water temperatures, fish are active for longer periods of the day and can typically be found in shallow water. A variety of baits and techniques will work during these times. When fish are active, crankbaits and spinnerbaits are usually the preferred choice. During the hot summer, the bite usually slows and fish activity is at its highest during early morning, late evening, and at night. Poppers, propeller baits, stickbaits, and flukes are good topwater choices during low-light conditions.

Crappie fishing is excellent year-round with jigs and minnows. During the spring spawn, anglers target shallow areas around vegetation. Other times of the year, fish are typically concentrated in deeper water around brush piles and creek channels.

Ebenezer Park is the only Sam Rayburn campground where horses are allowed.

3.22 Sam Rayburn Reservoir–Ebenezer Park

Location: Approximately 23 miles northwest of Jasper
Entrance fee: None
Season: Open year-round
Camping sites: 10 equestrian sites with 30- or 50-amp electric and water hookups; 20 basic sites (most only accommodate tents or small trailers)
Maximum length: No length restrictions
Facilities: Restroom with showers, dump station (small fee), drinking water. Equestrian sites have a paved RV pullout, hitching posts, covered table, and fire ring; corrals are also placed within the campsite area.
Fees per night: $$
Management: U.S. Army Corps of Engineers
Contact: (409) 384-5716
Finding the campground: From Jasper, take US 96 north approximately 12 miles to the intersection of Recreation Road 255. Go west on 255 approximately 8 miles to the park entrance road.
About the campground: Ebenezer Park is located on the south shore of Sam Rayburn Reservoir and is the only area on the reservoir where horses are allowed. The park has a designated swimming beach.

3.23 Sam Rayburn Reservoir–Twin Dikes Park

Location: Approximately 20 miles north of Jasper
Entrance fee: None
Season: Sites 1–10, 12–14, S-1, S-2, and S-3 open year-round; sites 15–43 open Mar 1 through Labor Day weekend; boat ramps open year-round
Camping sites: 6 sites with 30-amp electric and water; 6 sites with 30-amp electric, water, and sewer; 4 sites with 50-amp electric and water; 3 screened shelters with 30-amp electric, water, and sewer; 27 basic sites
Maximum length: No length restrictions
Facilities: 3 restrooms, 2 of which have hot showers; dump station
Fees per night: $$-$$$
Management: U.S. Army Corps of Engineers
Contact: (409) 384-5716
Finding the campground: From Jasper, take US 96 north 13 miles. Go west on Recreation Road, (FM 255) for 5 miles to the park entrance.
About the campground: Twin Dikes is a developed camping area located on the south shore of Sam Rayburn Reservoir and is home to a multitude of fishing tournaments throughout the year. There is a marina adjacent to the park (Sam Rayburn Marina and Resort), two boat ramps with eight launching lanes, and a group shelter.

3.24 Sam Rayburn Reservoir–Mill Creek Park

Location: Approximately 21 miles north of Jasper
Entrance fee: None
Season: Sites 47–110 open year-round; sites 1–46 open Mar through Nov
Camping sites: 105 sites with 30-amp electric and water hookups, and 5 sites with 50-amp electric and water hookups
Maximum length: No length restrictions
Facilities: Restrooms with flush toilets and hot showers, 2 dump stations (small fee), pay telephones
Fees per night: $$
Management: U.S. Army Corps of Engineers
Contact: (409) 384-5716
Finding the campground: From Jasper, take US 96 north 18 miles to Brookeland, then Loop 149 for 2 miles to the intersection with Spur 165. Go west 1 mile to the park entrance.
About the campground: Mill Creek Park is a highly developed camping area on the southeast shore of Sam Rayburn Reservoir. Amenities include a group shelter, designated swimming beach (small fee), playground, volleyball court, horseshoes pits, and boat launch.

3.25 Sam Rayburn Reservoir–San Augustine Park

Location: 10 miles northwest of Pineland
Entrance fee: None
Season: Sites 29–33, 50–70, and 87–100 open year-round; sites 1–28, 34–46, and 72–85 open Mar 1 through Labor Day weekend
Camping sites: 100 sites with water and 30-amp electric hookups, 5 of which are tent-only
Maximum length: No length restrictions
Facilities: Restrooms with flush toilets and hot showers, dump station (small fee)
Fees per night: $$
Management: U.S. Army Corps of Engineers
Contact: (409) 384-5716
Finding the campground: From Pineland, take FM 83 west 6 miles, then south on FM 1751 for 4 miles to the park entrance.
About the campground: San Augustine Park is a highly developed camping area located on the southeast shore of Sam Rayburn Reservoir on the Ayish Bayou tributary with a playground, designated swimming area (small fee), volleyball and basketball courts, horseshoes pits, courtesy dock, group shelter, and boat ramp with four launching lanes.

3.26   Sam Rayburn Reservoir–Rayburn Park

Location: Approximately 23 miles southwest of Pineland
Entrance fee: None
Season: Sites 26–50 open year-round; sites 1–10 and 55–65 open Mar 1 through Labor Day weekend
Camping sites: 16 with 30-amp electric and water hookups, 8 sites with 50-amp electric and water, and 22 sites without electric or water hookups
Maximum length: No length restriction
Facilities: Restroom with flush toilets and hot showers, 2 vault toilets, dump station (small fee)
Fees per night: $$
Management: U.S. Army Corps of Engineers
Contact: (409) 384-5716
Finding the campground: The park is located on FM 3127, approximately 23 miles southwest of Pineland. From Pineland, take FM 83 west 10 miles, then go south on FM 705 for 11 miles to FM 3127, then west for 1.5 miles and make a left into the park entrance.
About the campground: Rayburn Park is a developed camping area located on the north shore of Sam Rayburn Reservoir. The park contains four day-use picnic sites, a playground, and three boat ramps.

3.27   Sam Rayburn Reservoir–Hanks Creek Park

Location: Approximately 12 miles southwest of Huntington
Entrance fee: None
Season: Open year-round
Camping sites: 41 sites with 30-amp electric and water hookups; 3 sites with 50-amp electric and water hookups
Maximum length: No length restriction
Facilities: Restroom with hot showers, 2 vault toilets, dump station, pay telephone
Fees per night: $$
Management: U.S. Army Corps of Engineers
Contact: (409) 384-5716
Finding the campground: From Zavalla, take TX 147 northeast 0.25 mile, then turn north on FM 2109 and go 8 miles to FM 2801. Turn right (east) on FM 2801 and continue 2 miles to the park entrance. Follow signs to the campground.
About the campground: The park features a volleyball court, playground, and two boat ramps on Sam Rayburn Reservoir. Hanks Creek, located on the northwest side of Lake Sam Rayburn, has a day-use area with a swimming beach, group shelter, fishing pier, picnic sites, and play fields.

Gulf Coast

The Gulf Coast travel region is bordered by Louisiana on the east and Mexico on the west. Over 600 miles of coastline offer many recreational opportunities. The warm water of the Gulf beckons campers who want to swim, fish, sunbathe, build sand castles with the kids, surf, or just take a relaxing stroll on the beach. Get up early and drop a line off a pier or jetty, wade the surf looking for feeding fish, or head into the Gulf for some deep-sea fishing.

The Rio Grande Valley is the nation's number-one bird-watching destination, and most of the Texas Coastal Birding Trail stops fall within this portion of the state. Some of the birding opportunities include stopping at the Matagorda County Birding Nature Center or observing the endangered whooping cranes that winter at the Aransas National Wildlife Refuge.

From the campgrounds along the beaches that border the Gulf of Mexico to the inland sites such as the Big Thicket National Preserve, the region offers camping to suit everyone's interests, including hiking, bicycling, horseback riding, fishing, canoeing, and bird-watching.

Gulf Coast

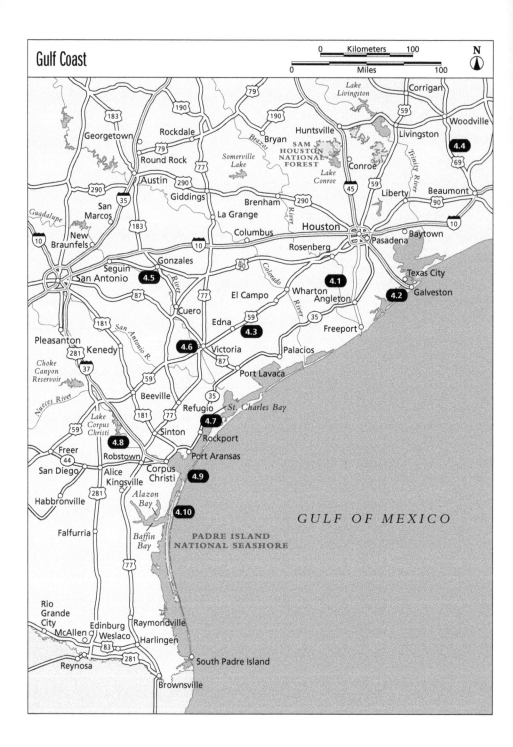

Kilometers 100
Miles 100

N

Lake Livingston
Corrigan
79
190
190
59
Woodville
183
Rockdale
Huntsville
Livingston
Georgetown
Brazos
Bryan
SAM
HOUSTON
NATIONAL
FOREST
4.4
79
Somerville
Lake
Round Rock
77
Conroe
69
Trinity River
Austin
290
Lake
Conroe
45
59
Liberty
Beaumont
290
Giddings
Brenham
290
90
San
Marcos
35
La Grange
River
Houston
10
Guadalupe
183
Columbus
Rosenberg
Pasadena
Baytown
New
Braunfels
10
10
Gonzales
90
Colorado
Texas City
Seguin
San Antonio
4.5
Wharton
Angleton
4.1
Galveston
4.2
River
87
77
El Campo
Cuero
181
San Antonio R.
Edna
59
35
Freeport
35
4.3
Pleasanton
281
Kenedy
4.6
Victoria
Palacios
Choke
Canyon
Reservoir
37
87
Port Lavaca
59
Beeville
35
Nueces River
Refugio
St. Charles Bay
Lake
Corpus
Christi
181
77
4.7
59
Sinton
Rockport
Freer
44
Robstown
4.8
Port Aransas
San Diego
Alice
Kingsville
Corpus
Christi
4.9
281
Alazon
Bay
Habbronville
4.10
GULF OF MEXICO
Falfurria
Baffin
Bay
PADRE ISLAND
NATIONAL SEASHORE
77
Rio
Grande
City
McAllen
Edinburg
Weslaco
Raymondville
83
Harlingen
281
Reynosa
South Padre Island
Brownsville

Northern Gulf Coast Region

	Campsites	Total Sites	Max RV Length	Hookups	Toilets	Showers	Drinking Water	Dump Station	Recreation	Fee
4.1 **Brazos Bend SP**	TRS	111	U	WE	F	X	X	X	HFRC	$$-$$$
4.2 **Galveston Island SP**	TRS	150	U	WEI	F	X	X	X	HSFBLC	$$$
4.3 **Lake Texana SP**	TR	141	U	WE	F	X	X	X	HSFBL	$$
4.4 **Big Thicket Nat'l Preserve**	T	*	N/A						HB	
4.5 **Lake Wood Park**	TR	22	U	WES	F	X	X		FBL	$$-$$$

* No established camping sites

Galveston Island State Park, located on the Gulf of Mexico, offers plenty of room for the RV or tent camper close to historic Galveston. Padre Island National Seashore has the longest undeveloped stretch of barrier-island beach in the world.

If you would rather be away from the beaches, Brazos Bend and Lake Texana State Parks and the Big Thicket National Preserve offer camping opportunities in inland parks. Big Thicket, a maze of swamps, rivers, and dense forests, offers primitive backpacking camping opportunities. Lake Texana State Park has campsites along Lake Texana, and Brazos Bend was voted one of the top camping locations in the United States.

4.1   Brazos Bend State Park

Location: Approximately 28 miles southwest of Houston
Entrance fee: Day-use fee (over age 12)
Season: Open year-round
Camping sites: 77 sites with electric and water hookups; 20 primitive equestrian sites; 14 screened shelters
Maximum length: No length restrictions
Facilities: Restrooms with showers, dump station (small fee for day-use visitors)
Fees per night: $$-$$$
Management: Texas Parks & Wildlife Department
Contact: (979) 553-5101
Finding the campground: From Houston, take US 59 south for about 28 miles to the Crabb River Road exit. At Crabb River Road, turn left and proceed about 15-20 miles to Brazos Bend State Park Road entrance on the left.

About the campground: The campground covers roughly 5,000 acres, with an eastern boundary of 3.2 miles fronting the Brazos River. Activities include picnicking, hiking, biking, horseback riding, and fishing. Six lakes are easily accessible to anglers, with piers located at 40-Acre, Elm, and Hale Lakes. There are at least three free interpretive programs and hikes offered every weekend. The George Observatory is located in the park and is open Saturdays from 3:00 to 10:00 p.m. For information on stargazing programs/passes and other programs, call the observatory at (979) 553-3400 or (281) 242-3055.

4.2   Galveston Island State Park

Location: 10 miles south of downtown Galveston.

Entrance fee: Small fee

Season: Open year-round, except during hurricane watch/warnings

Camping sites: 80 sites with 30-amp electric and water hookups, including 20 premium sites; 40 sites with 50-amp electric and water hookups, including 10 premium sites; 10 screened shelters (no pets allowed in this area); 20 overflow bayside sites with electric and water hookups (nonreservable)

Maximum length: No length restrictions

Facilities: Restrooms with showers, outdoor showers, dump station, shade shelter, picnic table, and fire ring at each hookup site

Fees per night: $$$

Management: Texas Parks & Wildlife Department

Contact: (409) 737-1222

Finding the campground: From Galveston, exit right off I-45 onto 61st Street and travel south on 61st to its intersection with Seawall Boulevard. Turn right and go west on Seawall (FM 3005) 10 miles to the park entrance.

About the campground: The park offers bird-watching, nature study, hiking, mountain biking, fishing, and unsupervised beach swimming. For summer play schedules for the Mary Moody Northern Amphitheater, call (409) 737-1744. Amenities include picnic sites, a fish-cleaning shelter, an interpretive center, a Texas State Park Store, a 0.25-mile self-guiding nature/interpretive trail, 4 miles of multiuse trails, and WiFi. A two-lane concrete boat ramp is located at Pirates Cove adjacent to the park.

4.3   Lake Texana State Park

Location: 6.5 miles east of Edna
Entrance fee: Small fee
Season: Open year-round
Camping sites: 86 sites with electric and water hookups; 55 sites with water only
Maximum length: No length restrictions
Facilities: Restrooms with and without showers, dump station, picnic tables, and fire rings
Management: Texas Parks & Wildlife Department
Contact: (361) 782-5718
Finding the campground: From Edna, take TX 111 east for 6.5 miles.
About the campground: Activities include boating, water and jet skiing, sailing on the main lake, swimming (no designated area or lifeguard), canoeing, hiking, and good birding and fishing. The park features a 1.5-mile hiking/nature trail (including 0.3 mile of granite gravel surface meeting ADA requirements); tree-shaded picnic sites (tables, grills, and water faucet nearby); a group picnic area with a pavilion; an amphitheater; a nature center and interpretive area for special programs; playgrounds; a double boat ramp; lighted fishing piers; a fishing jetty that is ADA accessible; and fish-cleaning facilities on the piers and near the boat ramp.

Blue catfish and largemouth bass are the most popular sport fish in the reservoir. The blue catfish are abundant, with frequent reports of large stringers, and flathead and channel catfish also provide noteworthy fisheries. Fishing for largemouth bass has recently improved. White bass provide excellent angling opportunities in the Navidad and Sandy Creek channels during the cooler months and in the main reservoir near the dam in the summer. Hybrid striped bass are usually found with schools of white bass in the deeper portions of the reservoir. Although crappie fishing can be tough in the summer, respectable catches are not uncommon during spring.

4.4   Big Thicket National Preserve

Location: North of Beaumont
Entrance fee: None
Season: Preserve headquarters open weekdays 8:00 a.m. to 4:30 p.m. (closed government holidays); visitor center open daily 9:00 a.m. to 5:00 p.m. (closed Christmas and New Year's Day)
Camping sites: Backcountry camping only
Maximum length: N/A
Facilities: Primitive camping
Fees per night: None
Management: National Park Service
Contact: (409) 951-6725

Finding the campground: From Beaumont, take US 69/287 north 30 miles to Kountze. Eight miles north of Kountze, take FM 420 east and follow the signs to the visitor center.

About the campground: Big Thicket is a naturalist's dream, a remnant of a primeval forest that's been called an "American Ark" for its biological diversity. The preserve contains remnants of a diverse ecological system and provides habitat for several threatened and endangered species. Once the inaccessible haunt of outlaws, Big Thicket is now plied by well-marked footpaths, boardwalks, and myriad canoe trails. The preserve consists of nine land units and six water corridors encompassing more than 97,000 acres. Big Thicket was the first preserve in the National Park system, established October 11, 1974. Campers must have a valid preserve-issued Backcountry Use Permit to camp in designated areas. Permits can be obtained at the visitor center or headquarters office.

4.5   Lake Wood Park

Location: 5 miles west of Gonzales
Entrance fee: Small fee per vehicle
Season: Open year-round
Camping sites: 19 RV sites with water, 30-amp electric, and sewer hookups; 3 sites along boat canal with water and 30- or 50-amp electric hookups (boats tie-ups available)
Maximum length: No length restrictions
Facilities: Restrooms with flush toilets, hot-water showers, tables, grills, fire pits
Fees per night: $$–$$$
Management: Guadalupe Valley Hydroelectric Division
Contact: (830) 672-2779
Finding the campground: Lake Wood Park is located approximately 5 miles west of Gonzales on US 90-A. Turn on FM 2091 south at the Lake Wood sign and head south for about 3 miles to the park headquarters building.

About the campground: Visitors to this 35-acre park enjoy a wide variety of well-maintained facilities, including picnic sites on the lakefront or in the shady pecan grove, a children's playground, tent camping areas, and full hook-up RV sites. The park store stocks food and fishing and camping necessities. Fishing, boating, and canoeing are popular attractions at Lake Wood. Enjoy convenient access to the 488-acre freshwater lake from the central dock facility, or take advantage of direct entry to the Guadalupe River from below the dam.

Southern Gulf Coast Region

		Campsites	Total Sites	Max RV Length	Hookups	Toilets	Showers	Drinking Water	Dump Station	Recreation	Fee
4.6	Coleto Creek Park and Reservoir	TR	58	U	WE	F		X	X	HSFBL	$$-$$$
4.7	Goose Island SP	TR	127	U	WE	F	X	X	X	HFBL	$-$$
4.8	Lake Corpus Christi SP	TRS	133	U	WES	F	X	X	X	SFBLC	$$-$$$
4.9	Mustang Island SP	TR	348	U	WE	F, NF	X	X		HSFC	$-$$
4.10	Padre Island Nat'l Seashore	TR	*	U		NF	X	X	X	HSFBL	$

* No developed campsites, but plenty of space for tent camping

As with the Northern Gulf Coast Region campgrounds, those in this area offer a choice of beach camping or inland campgrounds. Examples of inland camping are Coleto Creek Park and Reservoir, which is located on the banks of lakes used for cooling coal-fired power plants. In winter this lake can offer excellent fishing on the artificially heated water.

Coleto Creek Park consists of 190 acres, of which approximately 40 have been developed. In addition to campsites, the park boasts a boat ramp that provides the only public access to the reservoir, a lighted fishing pier, and a hiking and nature trail.

For the history buff, Lake Corpus Christi State Park overlooks an impoundment of the Nueces River, which was the disputed boundary between Texas and Mexico after the Texas Revolution. (The Rio Grande became the boundary at the end of the Mexican War.) Activities at the park include camping, boating, fishing, swimming, bird-watching, and hiking.

Mustang Island State Park is a beachfront camping and recreation area. Activities include picnicking, fishing, swimming, surfing, hiking, and mountain biking on 5 miles of open beach, along with excellent birding, especially during spring and fall migrations.

4.6   Coleto Creek Park and Reservoir

Location: Midway between Victoria and Goliad
Entrance fee: Small fee per vehicle
Season: Open year-round
Camping sites: 52 sites with water and 20/30-amp electric hookups; 6 pull-through sites with water and 20/30/50-amp electric hookups
Maximum length: No length restrictions
Facilities: Restrooms with flush toilets, dump station, BBQ grill and picnic table at each site, 4 camping cabins
Fees per night: $$–$$$
Management: Coleto Creek Power and Guadalupe-Blanco River Authority (GBRA)
Contact: (361) 575-6366
Finding the campground: From Houston, take US 59 south and travel 130 miles toward Victoria. Follow the Laredo and Goliad signs back to US 59. Turn right onto US 59 south and go 6 miles. On the right, a brown and white highway sign will direct you to Coleto Creek Park and Reservoir. Turn right onto Park Road, and go about 0.25 mile to the entrance. Check in at the two-story Spanish colonial-style building.
About the campground: The park has a four-lane boat ramp that provides the only public access to the reservoir, along with a volleyball court, horseshoes pit, marked swimming area, 200-foot lighted fishing pier, and 1.5-mile hiking and nature trail.

4.7   Goose Island State Park

Location: North of Rockport
Entrance fee: Small fee
Season: Open year-round
Camping sites: 57 sites with electric and water hookups; 45 premium sites with electric and water hookups; 25 walk-in (150 yards) tent-only sites
Maximum length: No length restrictions
Facilities: Restrooms with and without showers, dump station; tent-only and regular hookup sites have a picnic table, fire ring, and BBQ grill; premium sites have a picnic table with shade shelter and waist-high grill (no fires allowed in this area, except in the grill provided). The late arrival/over-flow camping area (nonreservable) is for self-contained units only (no tents allowed).
Fees per night: $–$$
Management: Texas Parks & Wildlife Department
Contact: (361) 729-2858
Finding the campground: From Rockport, take TX 35 northeast 10 miles to Park Road 13 and go 2 miles east to the park entrance.

About the campground: Although located on Aransas Bay, there is no swimming area at this park. The shoreline is comprised of concrete bulkhead, oyster shell, mud flat, and marsh grass. The main recreational activities here are camping, excellent birding, and fishing (the park participates in the "Loan A Tackle Program," which lends out fishing tackle to visitors). Other activities include picnicking, boating (motors allowed), nature study, wildlife observation, and photography. Guided nature hikes are held year-round, and guided birding tours are held January through April. Amenities include a fish-cleaning shade shelter; double-lane boat ramp; 1,620-foot lighted fishing pier with two fish-cleaning tables; group recreation hall with tables and chairs (no kitchen; capacity 50); playground areas; and a Texas State Park Store.

4.8   Lake Corpus Christi State Park

Location: 4 miles southwest of Mathis
Entrance fee: Small fee
Season: Open year-round
Camping sites: 25 sites with sewer, electric, and water hookups; 23 sites with electric and water hookups; 60 sites with water only; 25 screened shelters with electric and water
Maximum length: No length restrictions
Facilities: Restrooms with and without showers; dump station; picnic table and grill or picnic table and fire ring at each site
Fees per night: $$–$$$
Management: Texas Parks & Wildlife Department
Contact: (361) 547-2635
Finding the campground: From Mathis take TX 359 southwest for 4 miles, then turn on Park Road 25.
About the campground: Activities include picnicking, boating, waterskiing, fishing, unsupervised beach swimming, bird-watching, and hiking. The park has two fishing piers, fish-cleaning shelters, a group picnic pavilion (capacity 100), and two boat-launching ramps. One of the ramps is accessible only when the lake is full; the other is usually open, except when lake levels are extremely low (call the park for current conditions). There are no hiking trails in the park, but you can enjoy walking and biking on the paved roads.

4.9   Mustang Island State Park

Location: South of Port Aransas
Entrance fee: Small fee
Season: Open year-round
Camping sites: 300 primitive drive-up nonreservable sites on 1.5-mile beach; 48 sites with 50-amp electric and water hookups, separated from the ocean by sand dunes (50–75 yards from the water)

Maximum length: No length restrictions

Facilities: Hookup area has shade shelters and restrooms with showers; primitive sites (undesignated) have widely spaced convenience stations with portable toilets, cold-water rinsing showers, and bulk water supply.

Fees per night: $-$$

Management: Texas Parks & Wildlife Department

Contact: (361) 749-5246

Finding the campground: From Corpus Christi, take TX 358 southeast to Padre Island. Cross the JFK Causeway and continue 1 mile to the traffic light. Turn left onto TX 361 (previously Park Road 53) and go 5 miles north to the park headquarters, for a total distance of about 22 miles.

About the campground: The park comprises 3,954 acres with about 5 miles of beach on the Gulf of Mexico in Nueces County, south of Port Aransas. Activities include picnicking, fishing, swimming, hiking, and mountain biking on 5 miles of open beach, sunbathing, surfing, and excellent birding, especially during spring and fall migrations. Interpretive ecological tours are given on request. Facilities at the north end of the developed area (day-use only) include ample parking, portable toilets, and rinsing showers. Swim at your own risk in the Gulf of Mexico; there are no lifeguards. The primitive campsites are closed from time to time due to high tides; it is suggested that you call the park prior to arriving to check on beach conditions.

4.10   Padre Island National Seashore

Location: Southeast of Corpus Christi

Entrance fee: Moderate fee per vehicle

Season: Park open daily year-round; visitor center open daily 8:30 a.m. to 4:30 p.m. in winter, 9:00 a.m. to 5:00 p.m. in summer

Camping sites: Bird Island Basin: primitive RV and tent camping. A camping permit is required and is available at the Malaquite Visitor Center; reservations are not taken, but space is usually available. Bird Island is located on the Laguna Madre, approximately 4 miles from the visitor center.

Malaquite: 50 semiprimitive designated sites (26 tent/RV, 16 RV-only, 8 tent-only). Reservations are not accepted but campground is rarely full (during fall, winter, and spring, usually less than half the sites are occupied). Campsites are located less than 100 feet from the beach and have an unobstructed view of the Gulf. The visitor center is 0.5 mile south along the beach.

North Beach: primitive RV and tent camping. A camping permit is required and is available at the Malaquite Visitor Center; reservations are not taken, but none are needed as space is always available. Camping is permitted from the dunes to the water's edge (about 100-foot distance) and from the park's northern boundary to the northern barricade of closed beach (about 1-mile distance). Open to two-wheel-drive vehicles; however, beach conditions may vary with weather, and campers should always use caution to avoid becoming stuck in unexpectedly deep sand.

South Beach: primitive camping. A camping permit is required and is available at the Malaquite Visitor Center; reservations are not accepted, but space is always available. Camping is on the beach within 100 feet of the water's edge; there are no designated sites. The camping area extends from the dunes to the water and from the end of Park Road 22; 60 miles down to the southern boundary of the park at the Mansfield Channel. There are no roads; all driving is on the beach. The first 5 miles after the end of the park road are open to two-wheel-drive vehicles; the lower 55 miles are open only to four-wheel-drive vehicles. The beginning of the four-wheel-drive area is marked.

Yarborough Pass: primitive camping. A camping permit is required and is available at the Malaquite Visitor Center; reservations are neither accepted nor needed because space is always available. Located on the Laguna Madre, 15.5 miles south of the visitor center, access to this campground is possible only through the four-wheel-drive area of South Beach. To find the campground, drive to mile marker 15, then backtrack approximately 100 yards and look for a notch in the fore-island dune ridge. Drive through the notch to a caliche road, parts of which are sometimes flooded by marshes. Follow the road about 1 or 2 miles to the campground. Be aware that the flooded areas may be deep and that the notch through the dunes is sometimes filled with exceptionally deep, soft sand in which even four-wheel-drive vehicles become stuck occasionally.

Maximum length: No length restrictions
Facilities: Bird Island: chemical toilets. Malaqute: toilets, rinse showers, picnic tables, gray-water dump station, potable-water filling station. North Beach: no facilities. South Beach: no facilities. Yarborough Pass: no facilities.
Fees per night: Bird Island, $; Malaqute, $; North Beach, none; South Beach, none; Yarborough Pass, none
Management: National Park Service
Contact: (361) 949-8068
Finding the campground: From Corpus Christi, head east through the city on South Padre Island Drive (TX 358). After crossing the JFK Causeway and the bridge onto Padre Island, continue about 10 miles south on Park Road 22.
About the campground: Padre Island National Seashore, encompassing 130,434 acres, is the longest remaining undeveloped stretch of barrier island in the world and offers a wide variety of flora and fauna as well as recreation. Because of its location on a major migratory route known as the Central Flyway, approximately 380 species of birds have been documented within the national seashore—almost 45 percent of all bird species documented in North America. Bird Island Basin has a windsurfing area (ranked by *Windsurfing Magazine* as the best flat-water sailing site in the continental USA) and a boat-launching ramp.

South Texas Plains

Mild, balmy winter temperatures are what campers like most about the South Texas Plains. The topography in some places includes flat terrain broken only by mesquite and brush. In this region, history buffs can travel across parts of Texas that conquistadores once traversed on their explorations, and visit locations where Franciscan monks set up missions to Christianize and educate the natives.

Some of the more popular camping locations include Choke Canyon, Lake Corpus Christi, and Goliad State Parks. Falcon Lake and Choke Canyon Reservoir feature ample fishing and boating opportunities, while campers who like to stretch their legs can hike the trails around the two parks.

The waters of the Rio Grande form Falcon Lake, a beautiful 60-mile-long reservoir behind the dam. Falcon is a fishing paradise, especially for those seeking black and white bass, catfish, and stripers. The area is also very popular with bird-watchers, with the varied and interesting birdlife consisting of common resident birds, which range throughout the American Southwest, and many of the tropical species for which this is the most northwest outpost. There are also uncommon varieties such as the small green kingfisher and the varied bunting.

Bentsen–Rio Grande Valley State Park is the base camp for many birding adventures within the park and elsewhere in the World Birding Center system. Workshops and other seminars are offered periodically by World Birding Center staff and visiting ornithologists.

Lake Corpus Christi and Goliad State Parks have nearly 300 campsites between them. Goliad is on the San Antonio River and features a refurbished replica of Mission Nuestra Senora del Espíritu Santo de Zuniga. The mission was originally established in 1722 near Matagorda Bay and moved to its present site in 1749. It was the first large cattle ranch in Texas, supplying its own needs and those of Spanish colonial settlements as far away as Louisiana.

Choke Canyon State Park consists of two units (South Shore and Calliham) and is located on 26,000-acre Choke Canyon Reservoir, a water supply for Corpus Christi. The Calliham Unit offers camping, day and overnight equestrian use, boating, hiking, wildlife viewing, birding, and fishing. Seasonal guided bird walks are conducted on scheduled days. The South Shore Unit is a day-use-only park.

Goliad State Park is loaded with rich historical information. The park serves as a hub for visiting the Mission Espíritu Santo State Historic Site, the Presidio La Bahia, the Ignacio Zaragoza Birthplace State Historic Site, Fannin Battleground State Historic Site, the Goliad Historic District, and Mission Rosario State Historic Site. Activities include camping, picnicking, hiking, fishing, boating, swimming, and nature and historical study. The park is a take-out point for the Goliad Paddling Trail.

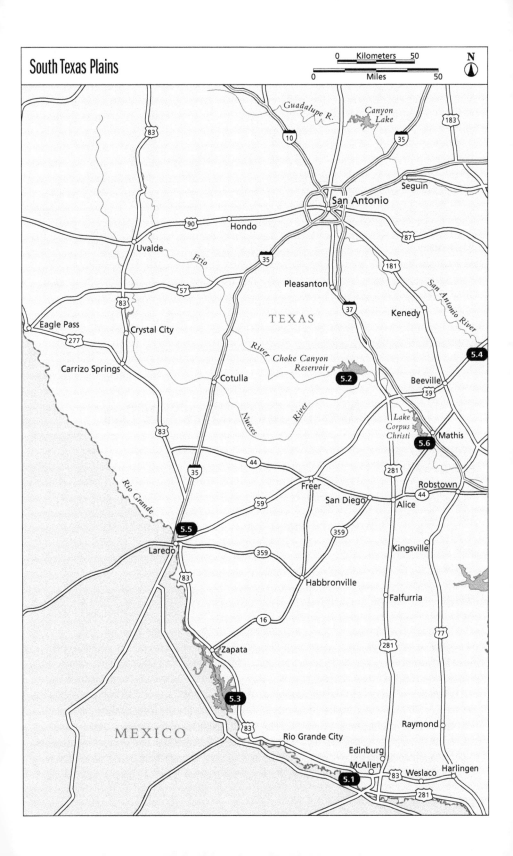

South Texas Plains

0 Kilometers 50
0 Miles 50

N

Guadalupe R.   Canyon
                Lake

183

83

10   35

Seguin

San Antonio

90   Hondo

87

Uvalde
        Frio   35

57   Pleasanton   181

83   San Antonio River

Eagle Pass   Crystal City   TEXAS   Kenedy
277   37

                                                              5.4

Carrizo Springs   River   Choke Canyon
                        Cotulla   Reservoir
                                                    5.2   Beeville
                                                                    59

                    Nueces   River   Lake
                                                Corpus
                                                Christi   5.6 Mathis
83

                        44   281   Robstown
        35   44
                    Freer   Alice
                    59   San Diego

                                        359   Kingsville
                                    359
5.5
    Laredo   359
                                    Habbronville

83   Falfurria

                        16   77

                    Zapata   281

Rio Grande   5.3

MEXICO   Raymond

                    83   Rio Grande City
                            Edinburg
                            McAllen   Weslaco   Harlingen
                                    5.1   83
                                                    281

South Texas Plains

	Campsites	Total Sites	Max RV Length	Hookups	Toilets	Showers	Drinking Water	Dump Station	Recreation	Fee
5.1 Bentsen-Rio Grande Valley SP	T	*	N/A						HC	$$
5.2 Choke Canyon SP	TRS	60	U	WE	F, NF	X	X	X	HFBLRC	$$-$$$
5.3 Falcon SP	TR	98	U	WES	F	X	X	X	HSFBLC	$-$$
5.4 Goliad SP	TR	58	U	WES	F	X	X	X	HSFB	$-$$
5.5 Lake Casa Blanca SP	TR	66	U	WE	F	X	X	X	HSFBC	$$
5.6 Lake Corpus Christi SP	TRS	133	U	WES	F	X	X	X	HSFBL	$$-$$$

* Undeveloped campsites only

5.1   Bentsen-Rio Grande Valley State Park

Location: Mission
Entrance fee: Small fee
Season: Park open daily 6:00 a.m. to 10:00 p.m.
Camping sites: Primitive sites by reservation only
Maximum length: N/A
Facilities: None
Fees per night: $$
Management: Texas Parks & Wildlife Department
Contact: (956) 585-1107
Finding the campground: Bentsen-Rio Grande Valley State Park is reached by travelling 7 miles west of McAllen on US 83 to Mission, exit on TX Loop 374 West and proceed 1.5 miles to FM 2062. Turn left (south) on to FM 2062 and proceed 2.7 miles to the park entrance.
About the campground: The crown jewel of Rio Grande Valley parks, Bentsen-Rio Grande Valley State Park well deserves its status as headquarters of the World Birding Center. Birders across the nation know "Bentsen" as a treasure trove of "Valley specialties"—those birds found nowhere else in the United States but deepest South Texas—and "Mexican vagrants," rare visitors from across the Rio Grande. The 760-acre park, together with over 1,700 acres of adjoining federal refuge land, promises year-round nature adventures in the richest birding area north of the Mexican border. Workshops and seminars are offered periodically by World Birding Center staff and visiting ornithologists. The park features daily tram service, four nature trails ranging in length from 0.25 mile to 2 miles, an exhibit hall, park store, and bike rentals. Access within the park is by foot, bike, or tram only.

5.2   Choke Canyon State Park

Location: Calliham

Entrance fee: Small fee

Season: Calliham Unit office hours are Mon through Thurs, 8:00 a.m. to 5:00 p.m.; Fri and Sat, 8:00 a.m. to 10:00 p.m.; Sun, 8:00 a.m. to 5:00 p.m. Park gates open at 6:00 a.m. and close at 10:00 p.m. year-round, except during public hunts. All South Shore visitors should vacate the park by 10:00 p.m. Campers who will be arriving after 10:00 p.m. should call the park before 5:00 p.m. to get the gate combination.

Camping sites: 44 RV sites with water and 50-amp electric hookups; 16 walk-in (50 yards) tent sites; equestrian/primitive camping area

Maximum length: No length restrictions

Facilities: Calliham Unit: restrooms with showers, dump station. Walk-in tent sites have water, tables, grills, fire rings, and lantern posts at each site.

    South Shore Unit: toilets, drinking water, shaded picnic sites on lake; day use only.

    North Shore Equestrian and Camping Area: equestrian/primitive camping (1,700-plus acres) with 18 miles of trails, accessed by a paved road across the dam from the South Shore Unit to North Shore. Four areas, with an 8-person minimum required for safety reasons. Area's terrain ranges from eroded, gently rolling brush to rugged and rocky areas that provide habitat for a variety of wildlife. A primitive camping fee is charged for each unit of 8, and a per-person entrance fee is also charged. Lake water may be used for horses; bring potable water. No sanitary facilities; however, toilets and drinking water are available at the South Shore Unit. Maximum 45 horses; no rentals or corrals available. Area closed one month each fall during hunting season; check schedule. Pack all litter and garbage out of the area for disposal; burying garbage is not permitted.

Fees per night: $$–$$$

Management: Texas Parks & Wildlife Department

Contact: (361) 786-3868

Finding the campground: Calliham Unit is located 12 miles west of Three Rivers on TX 72. South Shore Unit is located 3.5 miles west of Three Rivers on TX 72.

About the campground: Choke Canyon State Park consists of two units, South Shore and Calliham, and is located on 26,000-acre Choke Canyon Reservoir, a water supply for Corpus Christi. The South Shore Unit is a day-use only park (6:00 a.m. to 10:00 p.m.) and offers boating, fishing, picnicking, wildlife viewing, and birding. A six-lane and auxiliary two-lane boat ramp are available, along with lighted fish-cleaning tables and a lake overlook.

    The Calliham Unit offers camping, picnicking, day and overnight equestrian use, boating, hiking, wildlife viewing, birding, fishing, a lake beach, and softball and volleyball areas. Seasonal guided bird walks are conducted on scheduled days. The unit features a man-made 75-acre lake adjacent to the tent camping area, 2 miles of hiking trails, a mile-long bird trail, and a wildlife center that offers educational programs. Located outside of the park are four boat ramps: FM 99, Mason Point, Bracken, and San Miguel. Each has an honor box to collect fees.

5.3   Falcon State Park

Location: Falcon Heights
Entrance fee: Small fee
Season: Open year-round
Camping sites: 36 nonreservable sites with water close by; 31 pull-through sites with 50-amp electric and water hookups; 31 pull-through sites with 50-amp electric, water, and sewer hookups
Maximum length: No length restrictions
Facilities: Restrooms with showers (one ADA accessible), dump stations, group recreation hall with kitchen for day or overnight use; nonreservable sites have a BBQ pit, covered picnic table, and water close by; sites with hookups have a BBQ pit, fire ring, and covered picnic table.
Fees per night: $–$$
Management: Texas Parks & Wildlife Department
Contact: (956) 848-5327
Finding the campground: From Zapata, turn south on US 83 through Falcon for 2 miles. Turn west on FM 2098 for 3 miles to Park Road 46 and arrive at the Park Headquarters.
About the campground: Falcon State Park is nearly 577 acres (144 developed) located north of Roma at the southern end of the 98,960-surface-acre International Falcon Reservoir in Starr and Zapata Counties. Gently rolling hills are covered by mesquite, huisache, wild olive, ebony, cactus, and native grasses. Falcon Lake is an anglers' paradise, especially for those seeking black and white bass, catfish, and stripers. The area is also very popular with bird-watchers; varied and interesting birdlife consists of common resident birds, which range throughout the American Southwest, and many of the tropical species for which this is the northwestern outpost. There are also uncommon varieties, such as the small green kingfisher and the varied bunting.

Swimming, boating, and waterskiing are also enjoyed here. Amenities include 3 miles of hiking/mountain biking trails that make a complete loop around the park, a 1-mile self-guided nature trail with signs detailing plant life, a fish-cleaning shelter, playgrounds, and a Texas State Park Store. The park has a new boat ramp with three 24-foot lanes to an elevation of 269 feet and a single 24-foot lane to an elevation of 259 feet. The new ramp is in use when the lake is above 261 feet. The park also provides a temporary ramp for improved shore launching when the lake is below 261 feet; four-wheel drive is recommended for this ramp. Changing lake conditions can cause the temporary ramp to be unusable; if in doubt, contact the park.

5.4   Goliad State Park

Location: Goliad
Entrance fee: Small fee
Season: Open year-round
Camping sites: 24 RV/tent sites with electric and water hookups in Group Trailer Area; 20 sites with electric, sewer, and water hookups; 14 sites with water only
Maximum length: No length restrictions

Facilities: Restrooms with and without showers, dump station, picnic table, fire ring, and lantern holder at some sites
Fees per night: $-$$
Management: Texas Parks & Wildlife Department
Contact: (361) 645-3405
Finding the campground: From Goliad, take US 183 south 0.25 mile to US 77A.
About the campground: Goliad State Park comprises about 188 acres near Goliad in Goliad County. Situated within three ecological zones and located on the San Antonio River, the park offers a variety of flora and fauna blended with tangible remains of Texas history and culture. It serves as a hub for visiting the Mission Espíritu Santo State Historic Site (located in the park), the Presidio La Bahia, the Ignacio Zaragoza Birthplace State Historic Site, Fannin Battleground State Historic Site, the Goliad Historic District, and Mission Rosario State Historic Site. The park offers outstanding recreational activities and facilities, including picnicking, hiking (0.3-mile nature trail and 1.5-mile river trail), fishing, boating (no ramps provided for river access), swimming (a junior Olympic swimming pool, operated by the City of Goliad, is across from the park), and nature and historical study. It is also a take-out point for the Goliad Paddling Trail.

5.5   Lake Casa Blanca State Park

Location: Laredo
Entrance fee: Small fee
Season: Open year-round

Camping sites: 66 sites with 30-amp electric and water hookups
Maximum length: No length restrictions
Facilities: Restrooms with showers, dump station
Fees per night: $$
Management: Texas Parks & Wildlife Department
Contact: (956) 725-3826
Finding the campground: From Laredo, take US 59 east to Bob Bullock Loop (Loop 20), then turn on State Senator Judith Zaffirini Road.
About the campground: Lake Casa Blanca International State Park consists of 371 land acres and 1,650 lake surface acres. Attractions include picnicking, lake swimming, boating, mountain biking, and fishing.

5.6   Lake Corpus Christi State Park

Location: Mathis
Entrance fee: Small fee
Season: Gate open 7:00 a.m. to 10:00 p.m. Campers must check in by 10:00 p.m.
Camping sites: 25 sites with sewer, electric, and water hookups; 23 sites with electric and water hookups; 60 with water only; 25 screened shelters with water and electric
Maximum length: No length restrictions
Facilities: Restrooms with and without showers, dump station; screened shelters have picnic table inside, grill and/or fire ring outside
Fees per night: $$–$$$
Management: Texas Parks & Wildlife Department
Contact: (361) 547-2635
Finding the campground: From Mathis, 35 miles northwest of Corpus Christi, take TX 359 south for 4 miles to Park Road 25.
About the campground: Lake Corpus Christi State Park is a 14,112-acre park located in San Patricio, Jim Wells, and Live Oak Counties, southwest of Mathis. The present site of the park overlooks an impoundment of the Nueces River, which was a disputed boundary between Texas and Mexico after the Texas Revolution. (The Rio Grande became the boundary at the end of the Mexican War, officially making this area a part of Texas.) Once inhabited by Karankawa and Lipan Apache Indians, this area became the site of several settlement attempts in the eighteenth and nineteenth centuries. In 1858 Lagarto, now a ghost town a few miles northwest of the park, evolved from a Mexican settlement of grass-thatched huts. The town began a steady decline when its leaders rejected the building of a railroad through the community in 1887.

Park activities include picnicking (picnic sites have a grill and water), boating (motors allowed), waterskiing, fishing, unsupervised swimming, bird-watching, and hiking. Two fishing piers and fish-cleaning shelters are available, along with two boat-launching ramps. One is accessible only when the lake is full; the other is usually open, except when lake levels are extremely low. Call the park for current conditions.

Hill Country

This region begins in west Texas in Crockett County and stretches east to Austin, the state's capital in Travis County. Mills County is the region's northern point, and Kinney, Medina, and Uvalde Counties make up the southern border. The Hill Country is home to rolling hills that dominate the region, along with a breathtaking display of wildflowers along roadsides in springtime. Year-round lush green landscapes and plenty of splendid lakes and rivers beckon you to hike, take a dip, or cast your line.

There are almost two-dozen magnificent state parks here, most of which are located along lakes or rivers. Four parks on Canyon Lake, close to Austin, and four parks in the Amistad National Recreation Area offer opportunities for camping, fishing, swimming, hiking, and exploring. Campers at Blanco, Garner, Guadalupe River, and South Llano River State Parks can canoe or kayak the streams in or close to the parks.

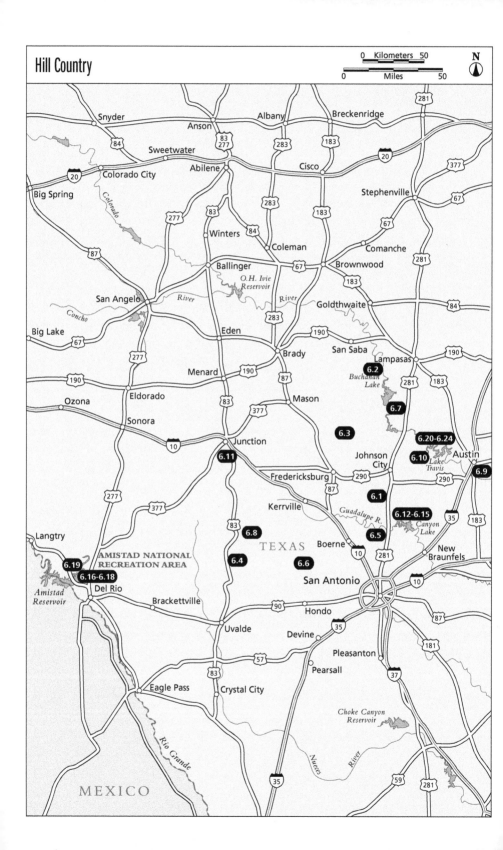

Austin and San Antonio Area

		Campsites	Total Sites	Max RV Length	Hookups	Toilets	Showers	Drinking Water	Dump Station	Recreation	Fee
6.1	Blanco SP	TRS	36	U	WES	F	X	X	X	HSFBJ	$$-$$$
6.2	Colorado Bend SP	T	38	N/A		NF		X		HSFBLC	$-$$
6.3	Enchanted Rock State Natural Area	T	106	N/A		NF	X	X		H	$$
6.4	Garner SP	TRS	407	U	WE	F	X	X	X	HSFCJ	$$-$$$
6.5	Guadalupe River SP	TR	90	U	WES	F	X	X		HSFB	$$
6.6	Hill Country State Natural Area	T	19	N/A		NF				HFR	$-$$
6.7	Inks Lake SP	TR	206	U	WEI	F, NF	X	X	X	HFBLJ	$-$$
6.8	Lost Maples State Natural Area	TR	70	U	WE	F	X	X	X	HSF	$-$$
6.9	McKinney Falls SP	TR	89	U	WE	F		X	X	HFC	$$
6.10	Pedernales Falls SP	TR	69	U	WE	F, NF	X	X	X	HSFRC	$$-$$$
6.11	South Llano River SP	TR	64	U	WE	F, NF	X	X	X	HSFBC	$$

Colorado Bend State Park offers the outdoor enthusiast access to primitive camping, hiking, and fishing. The park has nearly 16 miles of hiking trails and 14 miles of mountain biking trails, and offers guided walking cave tours and self-guided crawling cave explorations.

Enchanted Rock State Natural Area visitors enjoy primitive backpacking, camping, hiking, and technical and rock climbing. Convenient access to the Guadalupe River is available from the day-use area in Guadalupe River State Park. Hill Country State Natural Area offers around 40 miles of designated multiuse trails.

South Llano River State Park is home to white-tailed deer and the Rio Grande turkey. The bottomland represents one of the most substantial and oldest winter turkey roosts in the central portion of the state. Observation blinds offer visitors a glimpse of the turkeys moving to and from the roost.

6.1   Blanco State Park

Location: Blanco
Entrance fee: Small fee
Season: Open year-round
Camping sites: 17 sites with electric, water, and sewer hookups; 12 sites with electric and water hookups; 7 screened shelters
Maximum length: No length restrictions
Facilities: Restrooms with and without showers, dump station
Fees per night: $$-$$$
Management: Texas Parks & Wildlife Department
Contact: (830) 833-4333
Finding the campground: The park is located on the south side of Blanco, 40 miles north of San Antonio on US 281. Turn on Park Road 23 for 48 miles going west of Austin on US 290 to US 281, then south on Park Road 23. The park is only 4 blocks south of the town square.
About the campground: Blanco State Park comprises nearly 105 acres along the Blanco River in Blanco County. Early explorers and settlers used the park area as a campsite. Activities today include swimming, picnicking, hiking and nature study on the 0.75-mile Ira Caswell Nature Trail loop, boating (electric motors only), and fishing. Tube, canoe, and kayak rentals are available at the park, along with a group picnic area, playgrounds, and Texas State Park Store. The hilly terrain consists of cedar, pecan, and other trees. Among the animals seen at the park are nutria, mallard duck, raccoon, armadillo, and squirrel. Fish include perch, catfish, and bass, and in the winter rainbow trout are stocked.

6.2   Colorado Bend State Park

Location: Bend
Entrance fee: Small fee
Season: Open year-round, except during public hunts
Camping sites: 23 walk-in (10–40 yards) riverbank tent sites; 15 drive-up sites; primitive back-pack sites in the Windmill Area (minimum 1-mile hike); primitive backpack sites in the River Area (minimum 0.8-mile hike)
Maximum length: N/A
Facilities: Composting toilets; riverbank and drive-up sites have a picnic table, fire ring with cooking grill, lantern post, and potable water in the area. Windmill Area is about 6 miles from a compost toilet and water faucet; River Area is about 1 mile from a compost toilet and 1.3 miles from a water faucet. Carry in everything you need and pack out absolutely everything you don't use in backpack areas. Ground fires are prohibited everywhere in the park except in designated fire rings in the main camping area.
Fees per night: $-$$
Management: Texas Parks & Wildlife Department

Contact: (325) 628-3240

Finding the campground: From the intersection of US 281 and US 183 in Lampasas, take FM 580 west 24 miles to Bend and follow the signs 4 miles to the park entrance (2 miles of dirt road). From San Saba, take US 190 about 4 miles to FM 580 and follow the signs 13 miles to Bend, then follow the signs 4 miles to the park entrance. The headquarters and main camping area are 6 miles past the entrance on the dirt road (unmarked CR 442). *Note:* Access road subject to flooding. No gasoline service in Bend.

About the campground: Colorado Bend State Park, a 5,328-acre facility, is located west of Lampasas in San Saba and Lampasas Counties. The park offers the outdoor enthusiast access to hiking, fishing (which at certain times is terrific), swimming, mountain biking, birding, and nature watching. There are nearly 16 miles of hiking trails and 14 miles of mountain bike trails. When Lake Buchanan is near normal levels, the river is navigable from the park's boat ramp all the way to the lake, approximately 10 miles. This is a trip on slow-moving water through the beautiful canyon lands of the Colorado. On Saturdays guided tours are offered to Gorman Falls (reservations not required), which is also accessible by a day-use hiking trail (approximately 4 miles round-trip). The park also offers guided walking wild cave tours and self-guided crawling cave explorations. Reservations are highly recommended for the cave tours due to the limited number of people who can be taken at any given time.

6.3　Enchanted Rock State Natural Area

Location: Fredericksburg
Entrance fee: Small fee
Season: Open year-round, except during public hunts
Camping sites: 46 walk-in (25–100 yards) tent-only sites; 60 backpack (1–3 miles) primitive areas
Maximum length: N/A
Facilities: Walk-in tent sites have tent pads, picnic tables, fire rings, and water and restrooms with showers nearby; hike-in primitive sites have composting toilets. Backpack camping allowed in designated areas only; no facilities are available for vehicular camping of any type. Bring your own firewood.
Fees per night: $$
Management: Texas Parks & Wildlife Department
Contact: (325) 247-3903
Finding the campground: From Fredericksburg, take Ranch Road 965, 18 miles north to park entrance.
About the campground: Enchanted Rock State Natural Area consists of a little more than 1,643 acres on Big Sandy Creek, north of Fredericksburg, on the border of Gillespie and Llano Counties. Tonkawa Indians believed ghost fires flickered at the top of Enchanted Rock, and they heard weird creaking and groaning, which geologists now say resulted from the rock's heating during the day and contracting in the cool night. Visitors can enjoy hiking, technical and rock climbing, picnicking, geological study, bird-watching, and stargazing (minimal light pollution). Rock climbers must check in at headquarters, where route maps and climbing rules are available. A 4-mile trail for backpacking/day hiking winds around the granite formations, and a short, steep trail leads up to the top of Enchanted Rock (foot traffic only). The park also has an interpretive center and a Texas State Park Store.

6.4　Garner State Park

Location: Concan
Entrance fee: Small fee
Season: Open year-round
Camping sites: 149 sites with water hookups in New Garner area; 57 premium sites with water hookups in Old Garner area; 104 sites with water and electric hookups in New Garner; 57 premium sites with water and electric hookups in Old Garner; 16 screened shelters in New Garner; 24 premium screened shelters in Old Garner
Maximum length: No length restrictions
Facilities: Restrooms with and without showers, dump station, laundry facilities
Fees per night: $$–$$$
Management: Texas Parks & Wildlife Department
Contact: (830) 232-6132
Finding the campground: The park is located in Uvalde County, 31 miles north of the town of Uvalde, 9 miles south of Leakey, or 8 miles north of Concan on the Frio River. From US 83, turn east on FM 1050 for 0.2 miles to Park Road 29 to the new entrance.

About the campground: Garner State Park is nearly 1,420 acres (including 10 water acres of the Frio River) of recreational facilities in northern Uvalde County, located 30 miles north of Uvalde and 7 miles north of Concan. Visitors to the park can swim in the clear waters of the Frio River or scoot its rapids on inner tubes, and hike fascinating nature trails. On long summer evenings, young folks (and the young at heart) meet at the concession building for jukebox dancing every night during the summer season. Nearby is a miniature golf course, which is lighted for nighttime play. Meals and snacks are served in the concession building, though many families prefer to take advantage of the many camping sites and do their own cooking. A limited number of cabins are available for rent. The park also offers picnicking, canoeing, fishing, bike riding, and paddleboat, kayak, and inner tube rentals. There are 6 miles of surfaced road area for bike riding and day hiking, along with 5.5 miles of unpaved trails for hiking.

6.5   Guadalupe River State Park

Location: Spring Branch
Entrance fee: Small fee
Season: Open year-round, except during public hunts
Camping sites: 40 sites with electric and water hookups; 37 sites with water hookups; 9 walk-in (100 yards maximum) tent sites; 4 sites with electric, water, and sewer hookups
Maximum length: No length restrictions
Facilities: Flush toilets, showers, picnic tables, fire rings/grills
Fees per night: $$
Management: Texas Parks & Wildlife Department
Contact: (830) 438-2656
Finding the campground: The park is located in Comal and Kendall counties 30 miles north of downtown San Antonio at the north end of Park Road 31. It may be reached by traveling west on TX 46 for 8 miles west of the intersection of TX 46 and US 281, or by traveling eastward on TX 46 for 13 miles east of Boerne.
About the campground: Guadalupe River State Park is located along the boundary of Comal and Kendall Counties. The park has 4 miles of river frontage and is in the middle of a 9-mile stretch of the Guadalupe River. Visitors can enjoy a variety of outdoor activities, including canoeing, fishing, swimming, tubing, picnicking, and hiking. Opportunities also exist for bird-watching and nature study.

6.6   Hill Country State Natural Area

Location: Bandera
Entrance fee: Small fee
Season: Open daily Feb through Nov; open noon Fri through 10:30 p.m. Sun in Dec and Jan
Camping sites: 10 walk-in (maximum 75 yards in) tent sites; 6 developed equestrian sites with a capacity of 6 people/horses (combination); 3 nonreservable primitive backpack camping areas (total capacity 88) located 1.5 to 3.5 miles from the trailhead parking area

Maximum length: N/A
Facilities: Picnic tables, fire rings, chemical toilets, corrals and water for horses
Fees per night: $-$$
Management: Texas Parks & Wildlife Department
Contact: (830) 796-4413
Finding the campground: From Bandera, travel south on State Highway 173, go across the Medina River and continue for approximately 1/4 mile to Ranch Road 1077, turn right and go 10 miles on Ranch Road 1077 to end of the black top. Continue on the caliche road and follow the park signs to the park headquarters.
About the campground: Hill Country State Natural Area is located in Bandera and Medina Counties, 45 miles northwest of San Antonio. Hill Country is an undeveloped and secluded retreat tucked away in rugged terrain. Primitive and backcountry camping areas are available to both equestrians and non-equestrians. Approximately 40 miles of multiuse trails wind up grassy valleys, cross spring-fed streams, and climb steep limestone hills. Moderate fishing opportunities are available for catfish, perch, and largemouth bass.

6.7 Inks Lake State Park

Location: Burnet
Entrance fee: Small fee
Season: Open year-round
Camping sites: 137 sites with electric and water hookups; 50 sites with water hookups; 10 walk-in sites with 20-amp electric; 9 primitive hike-in (1.5 miles) sites
Maximum length: No length restrictions
Facilities: Restrooms with showers, dump station, backpack sites have primitive toilet on trail (ground fires prohibited, no drinking water)
Fees per night: $-$$
Management: Texas Parks & Wildlife Department
Contact: (512) 793-2223
Finding the campground: From Burnet, take TX 29 west 9 miles. Turn right then left on Park Road 4 and continue 3 miles to the park headquarters.
About the campground: Inks Lake State Park comprises 1,201 acres of recreational facilities adjacent to Inks Lake on the Colorado River in Burnet County. Amenities include WiFi, playgrounds, lighted fishing piers, a boat ramp, a 9-hole golf course with golf cart and club rentals, and a Texas State Park Store that offers groceries and rents canoes, paddleboats, and surf bikes year-round. The park also has 7.5 miles of hiking trails, including 1.5 miles of backpacking trails.

6.8   Lost Maples State Natural Area

Location: Vanderpool
Entrance fee: Small fee
Season: Open year-round, except during public hunts
Camping sites: 40 primitive hike-in (minimum 1 mile) sites; 30 sites with water and electric hookups
Maximum length: No length restrictions
Facilities: Restrooms with and without showers, dump station
Fees per night: $–$$
Management: Texas Parks & Wildlife Department
Contact: (830) 966-3413
Finding the campground: From Vanderpool, take Ranch Road 187 north for 5 miles.
About the campground: Lost Maples State Natural Area covers about 2,174 scenic acres in Bandera and Real Counties, north of Vanderpool on the Sabinal River. Visitors enjoy picnicking, sightseeing, hiking, photography, bird-watching, fishing, swimming, and nature study. Lost Maples has a Texas State Park Store and approximately 0.5 mile of nature trail and 11 miles of hiking trails. Be sure to stay on designated trails, because maples have a shallow root system and soil compaction from walking can damage the trees. Also, many natural hazards exist due to the steep/rugged terrain. Do not hike or climb on rocks or steep hillsides.

6.9   McKinney Falls State Park

Location: Austin
Entrance fee: Small fee
Season: Open year-round
Camping sites: 81 sites with electric and water hookups; 8 walk-in (100–200 yards) nonreservable tent sites
Maximum length: No length restrictions
Facilities: Flush toilets, dump station, picnic tables, fire rings
Fees per night: $$
Management: Texas Parks & Wildlife Department
Contact: (512) 243-1643
Finding the campground: The park is located 13 miles southeast of Austin off US 183. Take US 183 south 10 miles to the park entrance.
About the campground: McKinney Falls State Park in south Austin, Travis County, consists of about 744 acres. Activities include hiking, mountain and road biking, picnicking, fishing, and wildlife observation.

6.10   Pedernales Falls State Park

Location: Johnson City
Entrance fee: Small fee
Season: Open year-round
Camping sites: 69 sites with electric and water hookups; primitive camping area, accessible only by hiking or mountain biking for over 2 miles
Maximum length: No length restrictions
Facilities: Restrooms with and without showers, dump station; no pets or ground fires (self-contained fuel stoves only) in primitive area
Fees per night: $$–$$$
Management: Texas Parks & Wildlife Department
Contact: (830) 868-7304
Finding the campground: From Johnson City, take FM 2766 east 9 miles. From Austin, take US 290 west 32 miles, then FM 3232 north 6 miles.
About the campground: Pedernales Falls State Park, nearly 5,212 acres, is located along the banks of the scenic Pedernales River in an area that typifies Edwards Plateau terrain. Activities include river swimming, tubing, wading, and fishing; picnicking; hiking; mountain biking; bird-watching; and horseback riding. Over 150 species of birds have been seen in the park, and about a third of these are permanent residents. The wildlife is typical of the Texas Hill Country and includes white-tailed deer, coyotes, rabbits, armadillos, skunks, opossums, and raccoons. The park has 19.8 miles of hiking and mountain biking trails, 10 miles of equestrian trails, and 14 miles of backpacking trails.

6.11   South Llano River State Park

Location: Junction
Entrance fee: Small fee
Season: Open year-round
Camping sites: 58 sites with electric and water hookups; 6 walk-in (30–70 yards) tent sites
Maximum length: No length restrictions
Facilities: Restrooms with showers, dump station; walk-in sites have composting toilets and drinking water in the area. Both campsite areas have picnic tables and fire rings
Fees per night: $$
Management: Texas Parks & Wildlife Department
Contact: (325) 446-3994
Finding the campground: From Junction, take US 377 south 5 miles to Park Road 73.
About the campground: The 524-plus-acre South Llano River State Park adjoins Walter Buck Wildlife Management Area, south of Junction in Kimble County. Activities include picnicking, canoeing, tubing, swimming, fishing, hiking, mountain biking, and bird and nature study. The park features a day-use area near the river with picnic tables, waist-high grills, and composting toilets; oxbow lakes; 4 miles of hiking/mountain biking/nature study trails in the Turkey Roost area; and hunting blinds for wildlife photography.

Canyon Lake

	Campsites	Total Sites	Max RV Length	Hookups	Toilets	Showers	Drinking Water	Dump Station	Recreation	Fee
6.12 Potter's Creek Park	TRS	136	U	WE	F	X	X	X	FB	$$-$$$
6.13 Canyon Park	T	150	N/A		NF				HFRC	$-$$
6.14 Cranes Mill Park	T	46	N/A		NF				FBL	$-$$
6.15 North Park	T	19	N/A		NF				SFB	$-$$

Canyon Lake is dominated by steep rocky banks, isolated flooded timber, and clear water typical of a highland reservoir. The water becomes stained as one moves up the reservoir and into the river. In most of the lake, rock ledges, rock piles, steep drop-offs, flooded timber, and a few marinas provide cover for game fish.

The river portion of the reservoir is dominated by flooded timber, rock ledges, and laydowns. Largemouth bass is the most popular and most abundant sport fish in the lake. When the water level is high, largemouth bass anglers should concentrate on the flooded terrestrial vegetation.

White bass and striped bass also provide an excellent fishery. Stripers provide great angling because of their growth potential and strong fighting characteristics. Crappie fishing is generally poor, though occasionally good catches are made, especially along standing timber in the river. Angling for redbreast sunfish provides an excellent fishing experience for the family, and channel, blue, and flathead catfish are also present in good numbers. There is a small population of smallmouth bass, which tend to prefer the rocky habitat found in main lake areas.

Canyon Marina, 280 Marina Road (near Canyon Park), and Cranes Mill Marina, 16440 Cranes Mill Road, are located on the lake.

6.12   Canyon Lake–Potter's Creek Park

Location: North of New Braunfels
Entrance fee: Small fee for non-campers
Season: Open year-round
Camping sites: 114 RV sites with 50-amp electric and water hookups; 7 screened shelters with electric and water; 10 tent sites with 30-amp electric and water hookups; 5 family sites (each large enough for one family)
Maximum length: No length restrictions
Facilities: Restrooms with heated showers, lavatories, and flush toilets; dump station. RV sites have a covered picnic table; screened shelters have sinks with cold running water, ceiling fan, and picnic table; tent sites have covered shelter areas, cooker, and fire ring; family sites have a large covered table.
Fees per night: $$–$$$
Management: U.S. Army Corps of Engineers
Contact: (830) 964-3341
Finding the campground: From I-35, take exit 191 to FM 306, just north of New Braunfels. Travel west on FM 306 for 26 miles. Turn south on Potter's Creek Road and continue 2 miles to the park entrance.
About the campground: Potter's Creek Park is located on the northwest side of Canyon Lake.

6.13   Canyon Lake–Canyon Park

Location: Near Hancock
Entrance fee: Small fee for non-campers
Season: Open Apr through Sept
Camping sites: 150 tent sites
Maximum length: Not suitable for RVs
Facilities: Vault toilets
Fees per night: $ Mon–Thurs; $$ Fri–Sun
Management: U.S. Army Corps of Engineers
Contact: (830) 964-3341
Finding the campground: From I-35, take exit 191 north of New Braunfels. Travel west on FM 306 for 20 miles and turn left on Canyon Park Road
About the campground: Canyon Park is located on the north shore of Canyon Lake. For the bicyclist, the park offers the Madrone Trail, an 8.2-mile hike and bike trail. It is an intermediate- to advanced-level single-track trail with several sections that are fairly technical for most riders—drops, ledges, and lots of rock gardens. The trailhead parking area is located on Canyon Park Road approximately 1 mile off FM 306 on the north side of the lake. The Old Hancock Trail is a 3.5-mile multiuse trail along the north shoreline of Canyon Lake. The trailhead is located at the lakeshore end of Old Hancock Road, just off FM 306 on the north side of the lake. Old Hancock is also an equestrian trail, so please be respectful to riders on horseback.

6.14   Canyon Lake–Cranes Mill Park

Location: Just past the village of Startzville
Entrance fee: Small fee for non-campers
Season: Open year-round
Camping sites: 46 tent sites
Maximum length: Not suitable for RVs
Facilities: Tables, cookers
Fees per night: $ Mon–Thurs; $$ Fri–Sun
Management: U.S. Army Corps of Engineers
Contact: (830) 964-3341
Finding the campground: Cranes Mill Park is located on the Southwest shore of Canyon Lake off FM 2673, just past the village of Startzville. From I-35 take Canyon Lake exit west on FM 306; approximately 14 miles. Turn left on FM 2673 just after Guadalupe River crossing. Cranes Mill Park is located at the westernmost end of FM 2673 and South Cranes Mill Road.
About the campground: Cranes Mill Park is located on the southwest shore of Canyon Lake. Anglers and boaters can launch boats at Cranes Mill Marina. The marina is open 9:00 a.m. to 8:00 p.m., and the phone number is (830) 899-7718.

6.15   Canyon Lake–North Park

Location: West of New Braunfels
Entrance fee: Small fee for non-campers
Season: Open year-round
Camping sites: 19 tent sites
Maximum length: Not suitable for RVs
Facilities: Vault toilets
Fees per night: $ Mon–Thurs; $$ Fri–Sun
Management: U.S. Army Corps of Engineers
Contact: (830) 964-3341
Finding the campground: From I-35, take exit 191 to FM 306, just west of New Braunfels. Travel west on FM 306 for 18.5 miles to the park.
About the campground: North Park is a popular scuba-diving area.

Amistad National Recreation Area

	Campsites	Total Sites	Max RV Length	Hookups	Toilets	Showers	Drinking Water	Dump Station	Recreation	Fee
6.16 Governor's Landing Campground	TR	15	28		NF		X		SFB	$
6.17 San Pedro Campgrounds	TR	35	U		NF				HSFB	$
6.18 277 North	TR	17	U		NF				SFB	$
6.19 Spur 406	TR	8	U		NF				SFBL	$

Amistad National Recreation Area is the U.S. portion of the International Amistad Reservoir, formed on the Rio Grande along the border of the United States and Mexico.

The reservoir is known for excellent water-based recreation, especially boating and fishing, and is surrounded by a landscape rich in world-class prehistoric Native American rock art. You can see 4,000-year-old pictographs by boat or on foot.

Mexico requires boat permits and fishing licenses in its waters.

6.16 Amistad National Recreation Area– Governor's Landing Campground

Location: Near Del Rio
Entrance fee: Small fee for lake use
Season: Open year-round
Camping sites: 15 RV/tent sites
Maximum length: 28 feet
Facilities: Covered picnic tables, BBQ grills, drinking water
Fees per night: $
Management: National Park Service
Contact: (830) 775-7491
Finding the campground: Amistad National Recreation Area is located on the US and Mexico border near Del Rio, Texas and is between San Antonio and Big Bend National Park. The park is 150 miles west of San Antonio on US 90, and about 250 miles east of Big Bend via US 90 and US 385. Access to Amistad from the north or south is on US 277 and US 377.
About the campground: Governor's Landing has both a day-use area and a campground. There are eight picnic areas around the lake. Visitors can swim anywhere in the lake except in coves with

boat ramps or marinas. Governor's Landing is the only Amistad National Recreation Area campground with potable water.

6.17 Amistad National Recreation Area– San Pedro Campgrounds

Location: Near Del Rio
Entrance fee: Small fee for lake use
Season: Open year-round
Camping sites: 30 RV/tent sites; 5 tent-only sites
Maximum length: No length restrictions
Facilities: Picnic tables, BBQ grills
Fees per night: $
Management: National Park Service
Contact: (830) 775-7491
Finding the campground: Amistad National Recreation Area is located on the US and Mexico border near Del Rio, Texas and is between San Antonio and Big Bend National Park. The park is 150 miles west of San Antonio on US 90, and about 250 miles east of Big Bend via US 90 and US 385. Access to Amistad from the north or south is on US 277 and US 377.
About the campground: Hiking is permitted throughout Amistad National Recreation Area, including the five hunting areas. There are three established trails, at Diablo East, at the Pecos River, and the new Sunrise Trail connecting the visitor center and San Pedro Campground. Long-distance hikers can walk the shoreline, especially in the San Pedro and Spur 406 areas.

6.18 Amistad National Recreation Area–277 North

Location: Near Del Rio
Entrance fee: Small fee for lake use
Season: Open year-round
Camping sites: 17 RV/tent sites
Maximum length: No length restrictions
Facilities: Covered picnic tables, BBQ grills
Fees per night: $
Management: National Park Service
Contact: (830) 775-7491
Finding the campground: Amistad National Recreation Area is located on the US and Mexico border near Del Rio, Texas and is between San Antonio and Big Bend National Park. The park is 150 miles west of San Antonio on US 90, and about 250 miles east of Big Bend via US 90 and US 385. Access to Amistad from the north or south is on US 277 and US 377.

About the campground: Amistad National Recreation Area is a great place for boating. The park boundary extends 74 miles up the Rio Grande, 25 miles up the Devils River, and 14 miles up the Pecos River. Protected coves abound, providing superb fishing and ideal camping spots.

Amistad is an international reservoir—the United States-Mexico border is marked by buoys that follow the historic channel of the Rio Grande. You may boat on either side, but if you plan to boat on the Mexican side, be sure to have a Mexican boating permit. Some of the "favorite" catches at Amistad are smallmouth bass, largemouth bass, striped bass, channel catfish, and black crappie. Largemouth bass fishing has been doing extremely well lately in all parts of the lake.

6.19 Amistad National Recreation Area–Spur 406

Location: Near Del Rio
Entrance fee: Small fee for lake use
Season: Open year-round
Camping sites: 8 RV/tent sites
Maximum length: No length restrictions
Facilities: Covered picnic tables, BBQ grills
Fees per night: $
Management: National Park Service
Contact: (830) 775-7491
Finding the campground: Amistad National Recreation Area is located on the US and Mexico border near Del Rio, Texas and is between San Antonio and Big Bend National Park. The park is 150 miles west of San Antonio on US 90, and about 250 miles east of Big Bend via US 90 and US 385. Access to Amistad from the north or south is on US 277 and US 377.
About the campground: A boat ramp is located at this park. Depending on lake conditions, this ramp may or may not be open.

Lake Travis

	Campsites	Total Sites	Max RV Length	Hookups	Toilets	Showers	Drinking Water	Dump Station	Recreation	Fee
6.20 Arkansas Bend Park	T	*	N/A						HFBL	$$
6.21 Cypress Creek Park	T	*	N/A		F, NF				SFBL	$$
6.22 Mansfield Dam Park	T	*	N/A	P	F		X		SF	$$$
6.23 Pace Bend Park	TR	420	U	WE	F	X	X	X	HFRC	$$-$$$
6.24 Sandy Creek Park	T	*	N/A		F		X		HSFBL	$$

* Unimproved primitive camping only – no RV or tent pads

Lake Travis abounds with water recreation and is a true gem among Texas lakes. With its crystal-clear aquamarine water, the lake naturally attracts water-sport enthusiasts. Travis County maintains marina facilities, public parks, and boat ramp access. Hot weather makes it a destination summer resort for outdoor enthusiasts from around the state.

6.20   Lake Travis–Arkansas Bend Park

Location: Near Lago Vista
Entrance fee: Small fee per vehicle
Season: Open year-round for camping
Camping sites: Semi-developed
Maximum length: Not suitable for RVs
Facilities: BBQ grills, picnic tables; no drinking water
Fees per night: $$
Management: Travis County
Contact: (512) 854-7275
Finding the campground: Take TX 183 out of Lago Vista to FM 1431. Take FM 1431 south 11 miles to Lohmans Ford Road. Turn left on Lohmans Ford and travel 4.5 miles to Sylvester Ford Road. Turn left on Sylvester Ford and continue 1.5 miles to the park entrance.
About the campground: Arkansas Bend Park is one of the most isolated and untouched parks in Travis County. This peaceful 323-acre park lies on the north shore of Lake Travis near the community of Lago Vista. The park's 2 miles of shoreline offer opportunities for hiking, fishing, picnicking,

and lake access via an excellent boat ramp. Several inviting, shaded picnic and camping areas are situated along a bluff above a gently sloping, rocky waterfront. Overnight camping is available on a first-come, first-served basis; no reservations required. The gravel bars off the tip of the park's peninsula are popular anchorages for day and overnight sailors and boaters. Ground fires are permitted as seasonal conditions allow, but visitors are required to bring their own firewood. Cutting or gathering of firewood, including kindling, is not allowed.

6.21   Lake Travis–Cypress Creek Park

Location: Near Austin
Entrance fee: Small fee per vehicle
Season: Open year-round
Camping sites: Semi-developed
Maximum length: Not suitable for RVs
Facilities: Restrooms, BBQ grills, picnic tables, fire rings; no drinking water
Fees per night: $$
Management: Travis County
Contact: (512) 854-7275
Finding the campground: From the intersection of Ranch Road 620 and FM 2222, take FM 2222 (Bullick Hollow Road) west 2 miles. The park entrance is on your left, just before the intersection of Bullick Hollow Road and FM 2769 (Old Anderson Mill Road).
About the campground: Cypress Creek Park, an easy-to-reach small park within a half-hour drive of downtown Austin, is a favorite spot for boating, picnicking, swimming, and fishing. The main body of the park has a gently sloping waterfront. The boat ramp and cove provide easy access to the popular basin area of Lake Travis and other Travis County parks on the lake. Ground fires are permitted as seasonal conditions allow, but visitors are required to bring their own firewood. Cutting or gathering of firewood, including kindling, is not allowed.

6.22   Lake Travis–Mansfield Dam Park

Location: Mansfield Dam
Entrance fee: Small fee per vehicle
Season: Open year-round
Camping sites: Improved camping sites
Maximum length: Not suitable for RVs
Facilities: Restrooms, BBQ grills, picnic tables, drinking water, pay phones
Fees per night: $$$
Management: Travis County
Contact: (512) 854-7275

Finding the campground: From the intersection of Ranch Road 620 and FM 2222, travel south 4.9 miles. Turn right onto Mansfield Dam Road, just south of Mansfield Dam. The park entrance is on your left.

About the campground: As its name suggests, Mansfield Dam Park is located adjacent to Mansfield Dam on the main body of Lake Travis. The park serves as one of the primary access points for boaters. Other popular activities include picnicking, swimming, diving, and sunbathing. Set back from the water's edge, a central recreation area offers picnic sites, a playground, horseshoe pits, chess tables, and a panoramic view of the Lake Travis basin. Diving is almost as easy as stepping right from your car door into the lake. Dive stairs are provided, along with a wheelchair-accessible ramp and a courtesy dive lift to ease the trek from hillside to lakeside. Underwater amusement has been enhanced by the addition of four underwater dive platforms at various lake levels.

6.23　Lake Travis–Pace Bend Park

Location: 30 miles west of Austin
Entrance fee: Small fee per vehicle
Season: Open year-round
Camping sites: Over 400 nonreservable primitive sites; 20 improved sites with electric and water hookups
Maximum length: No length restrictions (sites are back-in only)
Facilities: BBQ grills, picnic tables, fire rings; restrooms, showers, and a dump station at improved location
Fees per night: $$–$$$
Management: Travis County
Contact: (512) 264-1482
Finding the campground: From the intersection of Ranch Road 620 and TX 71, take TX 71 west 11 miles to Ranch Road 2322 (Pace Bend Park Road). Turn right on Rand Road 2322 and travel 4.6 miles to the park entrance.

About the campground: Pace Bend Park is located in far western Travis County. With more than 9 miles of shoreline along scenic Lake Travis, Pace Bend is one of the most popular parks in the region, offering visitors a wide range of recreational opportunities. The west side of the park features high limestone cliffs and numerous rocky coves. The east and north sides offer more gentle, sloping shorelines with sandy and gravel beaches, providing easy access to the lake for families with young children and people with disabilities. Most of Pace Bend is easily accessible by vehicle from the 7-mile paved roadway that loops the park; however, the interior of the park is managed as a wildlife preserve and can only be reached by foot, bicycle, or horseback. Numerous trails lead into the hills and provide excellent views of the lake and the Hill Country. This area serves as home to a large number of white-tailed deer, raccoon, fox, and ringtail cat, along with dozens of bird species.

6.24 Lake Travis–Sandy Creek Park

Location: Volente
Entrance fee: Small fee per vehicle
Season: Open year-round
Camping sites: Improved nonreservable primitive camping sites
Maximum length: Not suitable for RVs
Facilities: Restrooms, BBQ grills, picnic tables, drinking water
Fees per night: $$
Management: Travis County
Contact: (512) 264-1482
Finding the campground: From the intersection of Ranch Road 620 and FM 2222, take FM 2222 (Bullick Hollow Road) west 2.5 miles to FM 2769. Turn left onto FM 2769 and travel 4 miles to the town of Volente. In Volente, turn right onto Lime Creek Road and follow it 6 miles to the park entrance on the left.
About the campground: Sandy Creek Park is located on one of the quieter coves of Lake Travis. This 25-acre park is an ideal spot for swimming, nature walks, birding, fishing, and, of course, camping. This park offers a serene, wooded environment away from the heavier boat traffic found on other sections of the lake. Sandy Creek is home to several rare bird and plant species, including the endangered golden-cheeked warbler. A hike along the wooded bluff and shoreline provides a good view of the lake. Ground fires are permitted as seasonal conditions allow, but visitors are required to bring their own firewood. Cutting or gathering of firewood, including kindling, is not allowed.

Big Bend Country

The Big Bend Country travel region includes the Davis Mountains, the most extensive mountain range in Texas. The range was formed by volcanic activity during the Tertiary geologic period, which began around 65 million years ago.

These mountains were named after Jefferson Davis, U.S. Secretary of War and later president of the Confederacy, who ordered the construction of the Fort Davis army post. After the war with Mexico, a wave of gold seekers, settlers, and traders came through the area and needed the protection of a military post. Indian bands also passed through the Davis Mountains. As west Texas settlements increased, raiding in Mexico and along the San Antonio–El Paso Trail became a way of life for the Apache, Kiowa, and Comanche. Fort Davis was active from 1854 until 1891, except for certain periods during the Civil War. In 1961 the historic fort ruins were declared a National Historic Site.

Campers utilizing the campgrounds in the area have the luxury of miles of trails with which to launch a trip into the backcountry and relive part of the history of the Old West.

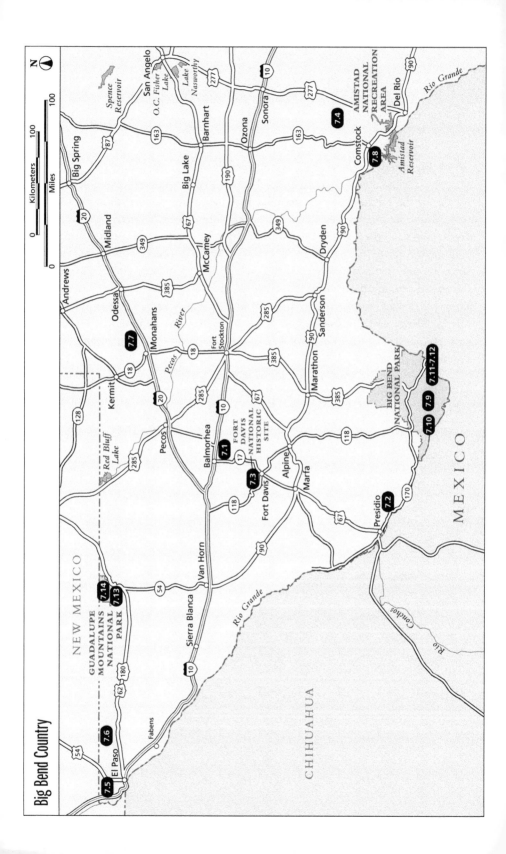

Big Bend Country

Big Bend

	Campsites	Total Sites	Max RV Length	Hookups	Toilets	Showers	Drinking Water	Dump Station	Recreation	Fee
7.1 Balmorhea SP	TR	34	U	WEC	F	X	X		S	$$
7.2 Big Bend Ranch SP	TR	11	U		F, NF	X	X		HFBRC	$-$$
7.3 Davis Mountains SP	TR	94	U	WESC	F, NF	X	X		HRC	$-$$$
7.4 Devils River SNA	TR	11	U		NF				HFBC	$
7.5 Franklin Mountains SP	TR	10	U		NF				H	$
7.6 Hueco Tanks State Historic Site	TR	20	U	WE	F	X	X	X	H	$$
7.7 Monahans Sandhills SP	TR	26	U	WE	F	X	X	X	HR	$$
7.8 Seminole Canyon SP & Historic Site	TR	31	U	WE	F	X		X	HC	$$

Big Bend Ranch State Park, over 300,000 acres of Chihuahuan Desert wilderness, extends along the Rio Grande from southeast of Presidio to near Lajitas. The scenic drive along the River Road (FM 170) follows the meanders of the Rio Grande and is among the most spectacular in the nation. Vehicular traffic in the park interior is allowed on the well-maintained, 35-mile gravel park road and several miles of designated four-wheel-drive trails.

Devils River State Natural Area's large size, approximately 19,988 acres, and remoteness support day hiking, primitive camping, nature study, mountain biking, and canyon tours. The park is a put-in point (no takeout) for canoes and kayaks. There are also primitive campsites by the river that are available only for canoe campers who have come downriver.

At Franklin Mountains State Park, two hiking trails are currently accessible off of Loop 375/Trans-Mountain Road. Work is under way for a trail network that will ultimately offer a 100-plus-mile system. Rock climbing, in McKelligon Canyon, is just one of the park's newest recreational activities.

Monahans Sandhills State Park consists of 3,840 acres of sand dunes, some up to 70 feet high. The park is only a small portion of a dune field that extends about 200 miles from south of Monahans westward and north into New Mexico.

7.1   Balmorhea State Park

Location: Toyahvale
Entrance fee: Small fee (over age 12)
Season: Open year-round
Camping sites: 16 sites with electric and water hookups; 12 sites with electric, water, and cable TV hookups; 6 with water only
Maximum length: No length restrictions
Facilities: Restrooms with showers, shade shelters
Fees per night: $$
Management: Texas Parks & Wildlife Department
Contact: (432) 375-2370
Finding the campground: The park is located 4 miles southwest of Balmorhea on TX 17, in Toyahvale. From I-10 westbound, take Balmorhea exit 206 to FM 2903 south to Balmorhea, then State Highway 17 west 4 miles to the park. From I-10 eastbound, take Toyahvale/Ft. Davis exit 192 onto Ranch Road 3078 east for approximately 12 miles to the park.
About the campground: Balmorhea State Park is located on nearly 46 acres in the foothills of the Davis Mountains southwest of Balmorhea in Reeves County. Visitors can enjoy picnicking, swimming, and scuba and skin diving (scuba divers must meet safety regulations). The park's main attraction is a large (77,053 square feet) artesian spring pool that is open daily and fed by San Solomon Springs. The springs also fill a cienega (desert wetland) and the canals of a "refugium," home to endangered species of fish, assorted invertebrates, and turtles. The pool differs from most public pools in several respects: the 1.75-acre size, the 25-foot depth, and the 72- to 76-degree constant temperature. It also has a variety of aquatic life in its clear waters. With a capacity of more than 3.5 million gallons, the pool has plenty of room for swimmers while offering a unique setting for scuba and skin diving.

7.2   Big Bend Ranch State Park

Location: Presidio
Entrance fee: Small fee
Season: Open year-round
Camping sites: 11 small, designated primitive campgrounds along FM 170 at Colorado Canyon, Madera (Monilla) Canyon, and Grassy Banks River Access in the backcountry (may be accessible to high-clearance vehicles only)
Maximum length: No length restrictions (backcountry may be inaccessible to large RVs)
Facilities: Showers and restrooms available by the visitor center at the Sauceda Headquarters; self-composting toilets at backcountry sites
Fees per night: $ (1–4 people), $$ (5–8 people)
Management: Texas Parks & Wildlife Department
Contact: (432) 229-3416

Finding the campground: From Presidio take FM 170 4 miles to State Park complex office.
About the campground: Big Bend Ranch State Park, over 300,000 acres of Chihuahuan Desert wilderness, extends along the Rio Grande from southeast of Presidio to near Lajitas in both Brewster and Presidio Counties. Embracing some of the most remote and rugged terrain in the Southwest, it encompasses two mountain ranges containing ancient extinct volcanoes, precipitous canyons, and waterfalls. The 19-mile Rancherias Loop Trail is available for serious backpackers. Trailheads are located at both ends of the loop along FM 170, near the Colorado Canyon River Access. The Contrabando Multiuse Trail is an easy-to-moderate 19-mile trail system. Trailheads are located at both ends of the loop, with the east end situated across from the Warnock Center. Campsites are designated, water must be carried in, and all wastes must be carried out.

7.3 Davis Mountains State Park

Location: Fort Davis
Entrance fee: Small fee
Season: Open year-round
Camping sites: 34 sites with electric and water hookups; 27 sites with sewer, 20/30/50-amp electric, water, and cable TV hookups; 33 sites with water (not all sites have their own water; several sites must share); primitive hike-in/equestrian (4 miles) sites
Maximum length: No length restrictions
Facilities: Restrooms with and without showers available at developed sites
Fees per night: $-$$$
Management: Texas Parks & Wildlife Department
Contact: (432) 426-3337
Finding the campground: From Fort Davis, travel 1 mile north on TX 17 to TX 118N, then west on TX 118N for 3 miles to the Park Road 3 entrance.
About the campground: Davis Mountains State Park, almost 2,709 acres in size, is located in Jeff Davis County, approximately halfway between Guadalupe Mountains National Park and Big Bend National Park. The upper half of the park, north of TX 118, has been designated the Limpia Canyon Primitive Area, a special-use area (small fee required). It currently includes 10 miles of backcountry hiking trails with primitive tent and equestrian campsites, a secured parking area, and a host campsite. Activities at the park include nature study, picnicking, hiking, backpacking, horseback riding, mountain biking, and interpretive programs. The park also features a playground, an interpretive center, 9 miles of hiking trails (not including the Limpia Creek Primitive Area), and a Texas State Park Store. A self-registration station is available at the headquarters for visitors arriving after office and/or park host duty hours. Campsite availability and status information is posted each evening.

7.4   Devils River State Natural Area

Location: Del Rio
Entrance fee: Small fee
Season: Open year-round
Camping sites: 7 primitive drive-up sites (4 people per site) with no shade (self-contained pop-ups, trailers, and motor homes are allowed); 4 primitive, nonreservable canoe sites (4 people per site), restricted to canoeists and kayakers who have come downriver
Maximum length: No length restrictions
Facilities: Restroom facilities are very limited; no drinking water
Fees per night: $
Management: Texas Parks & Wildlife Department
Contact: (830) 395-2133
Finding the campground: From Del Rio, go north on US 277 for 45 miles, then turn left on Dolan Creek Road and go 18.6 miles west to the park boundary. *Note:* Dolan Creek Road is a rough gravel road, and it is recommended that tires have a minimum rating of 8-ply to prevent flats and blowouts. The nearest gas station is 25 miles away and is not open all the time, and the nearest full-service station is 65 miles away.
About the campground: This remote park's large size supports day hiking, primitive camping, nature study, mountain biking, and canyon touring. Access to the river (1.5 miles) is by hiking, biking, or park tour only; no vehicle access permitted. The park is a put-in (no takeout) for canoes and kayaks. The nearest take-out point is about 10 miles downriver from the park, and only outfitters are allowed to take boats through these private lands. Lake Amistad is about 32 miles downriver from the park, and there is no cost to take boats out at the lake. The park only allows catch-and-release fishing; live bait is not permitted. No boats or motorized watercraft are allowed, only canoes or kayaks. All trash generated must be carried out of the park.

7.5   Franklin Mountains State Park

Location: El Paso
Entrance fee: Small fee
Season: Open year-round
Camping sites: 5 walk-in (25 yards) developed tent sites; 5 self-contained RV sites (no hookups)
Maximum length: No length restrictions
Facilities: Tent pad, picnic table, and grill at each tent site
Fees per night: $
Management: Texas Parks & Wildlife Department
Contact: (915) 566-6441
Finding the campground: The park is located on the northern edge of El Paso and has three primary access points. On the west side and from I-10, take the Canutillo/Trans-Mountain Road

exit toward the mountains and enter the park 3.8 miles from the interstate. On the east side and from TX 54, exit on Fred Wilson Road and turn west toward the mountains. The third primary access point is near the summit of the Trans-Mountain Road and is a parking lot with two trailheads.

About the campground: Overlooking the Rio Grande, the Franklin Mountains are the northern ramparts of the Paso del Norte (Pass of the North), leading from Mexico into what is now the United States. For thousands of years Native Americans—and for the last four centuries, soldiers, priests, traders, adventurers, gold-seekers, entrepreneurs, and just plain folk—have passed through the gap in both directions in an endless procession of expansion, settlement, raiding, and conquest. These people left their marks in the Franklins in the form of colorful pictographs on boulders and in rock shelters, and deep mortar pits (used to grind seeds) in rock outcrops near scattered water sources. Two hiking trails are currently accessible off Loop 375/Trans-Mountain Road, and work is under way on a trail network that will ultimately offer a 100-plus-mile system. Rock climbing is just one of the park's newest recreational activities, with established climbing areas in McKelligon Canyon.

The Tom Mays section of the park is the public day-use area. It has shaded picnic/BBQ sites, self-composting toilets, several miles of gentle hiking trails through the foothills of the Franklins, and primitive camping (tents only). Ground fires are not allowed within park boundaries, and there is no water or electricity in the park.

7.6   Hueco Tanks State Historic Site

Location: El Paso
Entrance fee: Small fee
Season: Open year-round
Camping sites: 17 sites with 30- or 50-amp electric and water hookups; 3 sites with water only
Maximum length: No length restrictions
Facilities: Restrooms with and without showers, dump station, walk-in picnic sites
Fees per night: $$
Management: Texas Parks & Wildlife Department
Contact: (915) 857-1135
Finding the campground: From El Paso, take US 62/180 northeast 32 miles and turn north on Ranch Road 2775.
About the campground: A unique legacy of lively and fantastic rock paintings greets the visitor at the "Tanks." From Archaic hunters and foragers of thousands of years ago to relatively recent Mescalero Apaches, Native Americans have drawn strange mythological designs and human and animal figures on the area's rocks. The site's notable pictographs also include more than 200 face designs, or "masks," left by the prehistoric Jornada Mogollon culture. Hueco Tanks was the site of the last Indian battle in the county, and these tanks served as watering places for the Butterfield Overland Mail Route. The site includes a historic ranch house that serves as the park's interpretive center, and ruins of a stagecoach station.

7.7   Monahans Sandhills State Park

Location: Monahans
Entrance fee: Small fee
Season: Open year-round
Camping sites: 26 sites with electric and water hookups
Maximum length: No length restrictions
Facilities: Restrooms with showers (heated in winter), dump station, shade shelters
Fees per night: $$
Management: Texas Parks & Wildlife Department
Contact: (432) 943-2092
Finding the campground: To reach the park, take I-20 and exit at mile marker 86 to Park Road 41. From Monahans, take I-20 east 17 miles to mile maker 86. Exit and take Park Road 41 north to the park.
About the campground: Monahans Sandhills State Park consists of 3,840 acres of sand dunes, some up to 70 feet high, in Ward and Winkler Counties, about a half-hour drive west of Odessa. Activities include picnicking, hiking, horseback riding, bird and wildlife viewing, and sand surfing. Texas Camel Treks are held at the park. Facilities include the new visitor/interpretive center built to ADA specifications, and an equestrian day-use area (about 600 acres) that has a staging area with hitching posts and water for horses.

7.8   Seminole Canyon State Park and Historic Site

Location: Comstock
Entrance fee: Small fee
Season: Open year-round, except during public hunts
Camping sites: 23 sites with electric and water hookups; 8 sites with water only
Maximum length: No length restrictions
Facilities: Restroom with showers, dump station
Fees per night: $$
Management: Texas Parks & Wildlife Department
Contact: (432) 292-4464
Finding the campground: From Comstock, drive west 9 miles on US 90. Park entrance is just east of the Pecos River Bridge.
About the campground: Seminole Canyon State Park and Historic Site in Val Verde County, west of Comstock, contains some 2,172 acres. Activities include picnicking, hiking, mountain biking, and nature and historical study. The park has an interpretive center, with exhibits relating to the history of the canyon area; 8 miles of multiuse trails for hiking and mountain biking; 0.6 mile of nature/ interpretive trail; and a Texas State Park Store. Fate Bell Shelter, in the canyon, contains some of North America's oldest Indian pictographs and is one of the earliest cave dwellings on the continent.

Big Bend National Park

	Campsites	Total Sites	Max RV Length	Hookups	Toilets	Showers	Drinking Water	Dump Station	Recreation	Fee
7.9 Chisos Basin Campground	TR	60	24		F	X	X		H	$$
7.10 Cottonwood Campground	TR	35	U		NF				HF	$$
7.11 Rio Grande Village	TR	100	U		F	X	X	X	HF	$$
7.12 Rio Grande Village RV Campground	TR	25	U	WES					HF	$$$

Sometimes considered three parks in one, Big Bend includes mountain, desert, and river environments. The park exhibits dramatic contrasts—its climate may be characterized as one of extremes. Fall and spring are usually warm and pleasant. Summers are hot, though temperatures vary greatly between the desert floor and the Chisos Mountains; May and June are the hottest months. Afternoon and evening rains often cool the desert from July to October. Winters are generally mild, though periods of cold weather, including light snow or ice, are possible. Winter campers should prepare for a variety of conditions.

Big Bend National Park is hundreds of miles from the nearest cities and transportation hubs. Distances between towns and services can be considerable, so always be sure you have plenty of gas, oil, food, and water for your trip. The park has four camper stores, but supply and selection can be limited. There are also small stores in the communities outside the park. The nearest major shopping areas (with grocery and hardware stores) are Alpine, Fort Stockton, and Del Rio.

7.9 Big Bend National Park– Chisos Basin Campground

Location: 28 miles from Terlingua
Entrance fee: Moderate vehicle fee. Small individual fee for a 7-day pass good at any park entrance
Season: Open year-round
Camping sites: 60 small, developed sites at Chisos Basin Campground; primitive backcountry sites in the Chisos Mountains and along backcountry roads
Maximum length: RVs 24 feet, trailers 20 feet

Facilities: Flush toilets, dump station, drinking water, grills, and picnic tables at developed sites
Fees per night: $$ (Chisos Basin Campground)
Management: National Park Service
Contact: (432) 477-2251
Finding the campground: Several highways lead to Big Bend National Park: TX 118 from Alpine to Study Butte; FM 170 from Presidio to Study Butte (then 26 miles west to park headquarters); and US 90 or US 385 to Marathon (then 70 miles south to park headquarters).
About the campground: Chisos Basin is surrounded by rocky cliffs, and many hiking trails are located nearby. The Chisos Basin Campground is rugged and hilly. The sites are small and most are not well-suited to RVs or trailers. The road to the basin is steep and curvy, especially at Panther Pass (the road's highest point), and the road into the campground is a 15 percent grade.

Camping is also available at primitive backcountry sites in the Chisos Mountains and along backcountry roads. A high-clearance or four-wheel-drive vehicle is necessary to reach most road sites. Big Bend's unpaved roads are generally unsuitable for RVs and trailers (check current conditions with a ranger). Overnight camping at any of the primitive road sites requires a backcountry-use permit, obtained in person at park visitor centers up to 24 hours in advance.

7.10 Big Bend National Park– Cottonwood Campground

Location: 28 miles from Terlingua
Entrance fee: Moderate vehicle fee. Small individual fee for a 7-day pass good at any park entrance
Season: Open year-round
Camping sites: 35 semi-primitive sites
Maximum length: No length restrictions
Facilities: Pit toilets (generators not allowed)
Fees per night: $$
Management: National Park Service
Contact: (432) 477-2251
Finding the campground: Several highways lead to Big Bend National Park: TX 118 from Alpine to Study Butte; FM 170 from Presidio to Study Butte (then 26 miles west to park headquarters); and US 90 or US 385 to Marathon (then 70 miles south to park headquarters).
About the campground: Cottonwood features grassy, shady groves along the river.

7.11   Big Bend National Park–Rio Grande Village

Location: 28 miles from Terlingua
Entrance fee: Moderate vehicle fee. Small individual fee for a 7-day pass good at any park entrance
Season: Open year-round
Camping sites: With 100 sites, the Rio Grande Village campground is the largest developed campground in Big Bend
Maximum length: No length restrictions
Facilities: Flush toilets, dump station, laundry and showers nearby
Fees per night: $$
Management: National Park Service
Contact: (432) 477-2251
Finding the campground: Several highways lead to Big Bend National Park: TX 118 from Alpine to Study Butte; FM 170 from Presidio to Study Butte (then 26 miles west to park headquarters); and US 90 or US 385 to Marathon (then 70 miles south to park headquarters).
About the campground: Rio Grande Village is the largest campground in the park and features shady campsites. Set in a large grove of cottonwoods, the campground is adjacent to the Rio Grande at an elevation of 1,850 feet.

7.12   Big Bend National Park– Rio Grande Village RV Campground

Location: 28 miles from Terlingua
Entrance fee: N/A
Season: Open year-round
Camping sites: 25 sites
Maximum length: No length restrictions
Facilities: Water, sewer and electric hookups
Fees per night: $$$
Management: Forever Resorts, Inc.
Contact: (432) 477-2293
Finding the campground: Several highways lead to Big Bend National Park: TX 118 from Alpine to Study Butte; FM 170 from Presidio to Study Butte (then 26 miles west to park headquarters); and US 90 or US 385 to Marathon (then 70 miles south to park headquarters).
About this campground: The Rio Grande Village campground is the largest developed campground in Big Bend. Set in a large grove of cottonwoods, the campground is adjacent to the Rio Grande with an elevation of 1,850 feet.

Guadalupe Mountains National Park

	Campsites	Total Sites	Max RV Length	Hookups	Toilets	Showers	Drinking Water	Dump Station	Recreation	Fee
7.13 Pine Springs Campground	TR	32	U	W	F		X		HR	$
7.14 Dog Canyon Campground	TR	13	U	W	F		X		H	$

At Guadalupe Mountains National Park, a hiker's paradise, you will find more than 80 miles of trails that meander through woodland canyons and lush riparian springs, or zigzag up steep switchbacks directly into the park's rugged wilderness. Trails range in difficulty from easy to strenuous, and many are rocky, often steep, and rugged. They lead to Guadalupe Peak, around the base of El Capitan, up into the high country, and into McKittrick Canyon. Self-guided nature trails are located at McKittrick Canyon, Dog Canyon, and at the headquarters visitor center.

The park is a wonderful place to view fossils and learn about Permian geology, enjoy bird-watching and wildlife observation, delve into nature photography, or partake of unlimited opportunities for stargazing under pristine night skies.

The closest place to find ice, groceries, showers, and lodging is 35 miles east in White's City, New Mexico. Gasoline is also available there, or 32 miles west of the park on US 62/180. Consider the park's remote location and plan your trip wisely, bringing everything with you.

7.13 Guadalupe Mountains National Park– Pine Springs Campground

Location: Salt Flat
Entrance fee: Small fee
Season: Open year-round
Camping sites: 20 basic tent sites; 12 basic RV sites in parking area
Maximum length: No length restrictions
Facilities: Restrooms, drinking water
Fees per night: $
Management: National Park Service
Contact: (915) 828-3251

Finding the campground: Guadalupe Mountains National Park is located 110 miles east of El Paso, TX, via US 62/180; 55 miles southwest of Carlsbad, NM, via US 62/180; 65 miles north of Van Horn, TX, via TX 54 to US 62/180.

About the campground: This park is a hiker's paradise. You will find more than 80 miles of trails that meander through woodland canyons and lush riparian springs, or zigzag up steep switchbacks directly into the park's rugged wilderness. Many trails are available for horseback riding if you bring your own stock.

7.14 Guadalupe Mountains National Park– Dog Canyon Campground

Location: Salt Flat
Entrance fee: Small fee
Season: Open year-round
Camping sites: 9 basic tent sites; 4 basic RV sites
Maximum length: No length restrictions
Facilities: Restrooms, drinking water
Fees per night: $
Management: National Park Service
Contact: (505) 981-2418
Finding the campground: Dog Canyon is located on the north side of the park and can be accessed via NM 137, 70 miles from Carlsbad, NM. You can also reach Dog Canyon by exiting US 62/180, 22 miles south of the park on FM 1576 to NM 137. *Note:* 31 miles of this route is a gravel/dirt road.

About the campground: Visitors may generally expect relatively hot summers; calm, mild autumn weather; and cool to cold weather in winter and early spring. Snowstorms, freezing rain, or fog may occur in winter and early spring. Frequent high-wind warnings are issued winter through spring, and late-summer monsoons produce thunderstorms. You can expect cool nights, even in summer.

Camping Tips

First Aid

When you go camping, make sure your first-aid kit contains at least the following:

- Band-Aids
- mole skin
- various sterile gauze and dressings
- white surgical tape
- an Ace bandage
- an antihistamine
- aspirin
- Betadine solution
- a first-aid book
- Tums

- tweezers
- scissors
- antibacterial wipes
- triple-antibiotic ointment
- plastic gloves
- sterile cotton tip applicators
- syrup of ipecac (to induce vomiting)
- thermometer
- wire splint

Here are a few tips for dealing with and hopefully preventing certain ailments.

Sunburn. Take along sunscreen or sun block, protective clothing, and a wide-brimmed hat. If you do get a sunburn, treat the area with aloe vera gel, and protect the area from further sun exposure. At higher elevations, the sun's radiation can be particularly damaging to skin. Remember that your eyes are vulnerable to this radiation as well. Sunglasses can be a good way to prevent headaches and permanent eye damage from the sun, especially in places where light-colored rock or patches of snow reflect light up in your face.

Blisters. Be prepared to take care of these camp-spoilers by carrying moleskin (a lightly padded adhesive), gauze and tape, or adhesive bandages. An effective way to apply moleskin is to cut out a circle of moleskin and remove the center—like a doughnut—and place it over the blistered area. Cutting the center out will reduce the pressure applied to the sensitive skin. Other products can help you combat blisters. Some are applied to suspicious hot spots before a blister forms to help decrease friction to that area, while others are applied to the blister after it has popped to help prevent further irritation.

Insect bites and stings. You can treat most insect bites and stings by applying hydrocortisone 1% cream topically and taking a pain medication such as ibuprofen or acetaminophen to reduce swelling. If you forgot to pack these items, a cold compress or a paste of mud and ashes can sometimes assuage the itching and discomfort. Remove any stingers by using tweezers or scraping the area with your fingernail or a knife blade. Don't pinch the area as you'll only spread the venom.

Some campers are highly sensitive to bites and stings and may have a serious allergic reaction that can be life threatening. Symptoms of a serious allergic reaction can include wheezing, an asthmatic attack, and shock. The treatment for this severe type of reaction is epinephrine. If you know that you are sensitive to bites and stings, carry a pre-packaged kit of epinephrine, which can be obtained only by prescription from your doctor.

Ticks. Ticks can carry diseases such as Rocky Mountain spotted fever and Lyme disease. The best defense is, of course, prevention. If you know you're going to be camping in an area littered with ticks, wear long pants and a long sleeved shirt. You can apply a permethrin repellent to your clothing and a Deet repellent to exposed skin. At the end of your hike, do a spot check for ticks (and insects in general). If you do find a tick, coat the insect with petroleum jelly or tree sap to cut off its air supply. The tick should release its hold, but if it doesn't, grab the head of the tick firmly—with a pair of tweezers if you have them—and gently pull it away from the skin with a twisting motion. Sometimes the mouth parts linger, embedded in your skin. If this happens, try to remove them with a disinfected needle. Clean the affected area with an antibacterial cleanser and then apply triple antibiotic ointment. Monitor the area for a few days. If irritation persists or a white spot develops, see a doctor for possible infection.

Poison ivy, oak, and sumac. These skin irritants can be found most anywhere in North America and come in the form of a bush or a vine, having leaflets in groups of three, five, seven, or nine. Learn how to spot the plants. The oil they secrete can cause an allergic reaction in the form of blisters, usually about twelve hours after exposure. The itchy rash can last from ten days to several weeks. The best defense against these irritants is to wear clothing that covers the arms, legs and torso. For summer, zip-off cargo pants come in handy. There are also nonprescription lotions you can apply to exposed skin that guard against the effects of poison ivy/oak/sumac and can be washed off with soap and water. If you think you were in contact with the plants, after hiking (or even on the trail during longer hikes) wash with soap and water. Taking a hot shower with soap after you return home from your hike will also help to remove any lingering oil from your skin. Should you contract a rash from any of these plants, use an antihistamine to reduce the itching. If the rash is localized, create a light bleach/water wash to dry up the area. If the rash has spread, either tough it out or see your doctor about getting a dose of cortisone (available both orally and by injection).

Snakebites. Snakebites are rare in North America. Unless startled or provoked, the majority of snakes will not bite. If you are wise to their habitats and keep a careful eye on the trail, you should be just fine. When stepping over logs, first step on the log, making sure you can see what's on the other side before stepping down. Though your chances of being struck are slim, it's wise to know what to do in the event you are.

If a nonpoisonous snake bites you, allow the wound to bleed a small amount and then cleanse the wounded area with a Betadine solution (10% povidone iodine). Rinse the wound with clean water (preferably) or fresh urine (it might sound ugly, but it's sterile). Once the area is clean, cover it with triple antibiotic ointment and a clean bandage. Remember, most residual damage from snakebites, poisonous or otherwise, comes from infection, not the snake's venom. Keep the area as clean as possible and get medical attention immediately.

If you are bitten by a poisonous snake, remove the toxin with a suctioning device, found in a snakebite kit. If you do not have such a device, squeeze the wound—DO NOT use your mouth for suction, as the venom will enter your bloodstream through the vessels under the tongue and head straight for your heart. Then, clean the wound just as you would a nonpoisonous bite. Tie a clean band of cloth snuggly around the afflicted appendage, about an inch or so above the bite (or the rim of the swelling). This is NOT a tourniquet—you want to simply slow the blood flow, not cut it off. Loosen the band if numbness ensues. Remove the band for a minute and reapply a little higher every ten minutes.

If it is your friend who's been bitten, treat him or her for shock—make the person comfortable, have him or her lie down, elevate the legs, and keep him or her warm. Avoid applying anything cold to the bite wound. Immobilize the affected area and remove any constricting items such as rings, watches, or restrictive clothing—swelling may occur. Once your friend is stable and relatively calm, hike out to get help. The victim should get treatment within twelve hours, ideally, which usually consists of a tetanus shot, antivenin, and antibiotics.

If you are alone and struck by a poisonous snake, stay calm. Hysteria will only quicken the venom's spread. Follow the procedure above, and do your best to reach help. When hiking out, don't run—you'll only increase the flow of blood throughout your system. Instead, walk calmly.

Dehydration. Have you ever hiked in hot weather and had a roaring headache and felt fatigued after only a few miles? More than likely you were dehydrated. Symptoms of dehydration include fatigue, headache, and decreased coordination and judgment. When you are hiking, your body's rate of fluid loss depends on the outside temperature, humidity, altitude, and your activity level. On average, a hiker walking in warm weather will lose four liters of fluid a day. That fluid loss is easily replaced by normal consumption of liquids and food. However, if a hiker is walking briskly in hot, dry weather and hauling a heavy pack, he or she can lose one to three liters of water an hour. It's important to always carry plenty of water and to stop often and drink fluids regularly, even if you aren't thirsty.

Heat exhaustion is the result of a loss of large amounts of electrolytes and often occurs if a hiker is dehydrated and has been under heavy exertion. Common symptoms of heat exhaustion include cramping, exhaustion, fatigue, lightheadedness, and nausea. You can treat heat exhaustion by getting out of the sun and drinking an electrolyte solution made up of one teaspoon of salt and one tablespoon of sugar dissolved in a liter of water. Drink this solution slowly over a period of one hour. Drinking plenty of fluids (preferably an electrolyte solution/sports drink) can prevent heat exhaustion. Avoid hiking during the hottest parts of the day, and wear breathable clothing, a wide-brimmed hat, and sunglasses.

Hypothermia is one of the biggest dangers in the backcountry, especially for day hikers in the summertime. That may sound strange, but imagine starting out on a hike in midsummer when it's sunny and 80 degrees out. You're clad in nylon shorts and a cotton T-shirt. About halfway through your hike, the sky begins to cloud up, and in the next hour a light drizzle begins to fall and the wind starts to pick up. Before you know it, you are soaking wet and shivering—the perfect recipe for hypothermia. More advanced signs include decreased coordination, slurred speech, and blurred vision. When a victim's temperature falls below 92 degrees, the blood pressure and pulse plummet, possibly leading to coma and death.

To avoid hypothermia, always bring a windproof/rainproof shell, a fleece jacket, tights made of a breathable, synthetic fiber, gloves, and hat when you are hiking in the mountains. Learn to adjust your clothing layers based on the temperature. If you are climbing uphill at a moderate pace you will stay warm, but when you stop for a break you'll become cold quickly, unless you add more layers of clothing.

If a hiker is showing advanced signs of hypothermia, dress him or her in dry clothes and make sure he or she is wearing a hat and gloves. Place the person in a sleeping bag in a tent or shelter that will protect him or her from the wind and other elements. Give the person warm fluids to drink and keep him awake.

Frostbite. When the mercury dips below 32 degrees, your extremities begin to chill. If a persistent chill attacks a localized area, say, your hands or your toes, the circulatory system reacts by cutting off blood flow to the affected area—the idea being to protect and preserve the body's overall temperature. And so it's death by attrition for the affected area. Ice crystals start to form from the water in the cells of the neglected tissue. Deprived of heat, nourishment, and now water, the tissue literally starves. This is frostbite.

Prevention is your best defense against this situation. Most prone to frostbite are your face, hands, and feet, so protect these areas well. Wool is the material of choice because it provides ample air space for insulation and draws moisture away from the skin. Synthetic fabrics, however, have recently made great strides in the cold weather clothing market. Do your research. A pair of light silk liners under your regular gloves is a good trick for keeping warm. They afford some additional warmth, but more importantly they'll allow you to remove your mitts for tedious work without exposing the skin.

If your feet or hands start to feel cold or numb due to the elements, warm them as quickly as possible. Place cold hands under your armpits or bury them in your crotch. If your feet are cold, change your socks. If there's plenty of room in your boots, add another pair of socks. Do remember, though, that constricting your feet in tight boots can restrict blood flow and actually make your feet colder more quickly. Your socks need to have breathing room if they're going to be effective. Dead air provides insulation. If your face is cold, place your warm hands over your face, or simply wear a head stocking.

Should your skin go numb and start to appear white and waxy, chances are you've got or are developing frostbite. Don't try to thaw the area unless you can maintain the warmth. In other words, don't stop to warm up your frostbitten feet only to head back on the trail. You'll do more damage than good. Tests have shown that hikers who walked on thawed feet did more harm, and endured more pain, than hikers who left the affected areas alone. Do your best to get out of the cold entirely and seek medical attention—which usually consists of performing a rapid rewarming in water for twenty to thirty minutes.

The overall objective in preventing both hypothermia and frostbite is to keep the body's core warm. Protect key areas where heat escapes, like the top of the head, and maintain the proper nutrition level. Foods that are high in calories aid the body in producing heat. Never smoke or drink when you're in situations where the cold is threatening. By affecting blood flow, these activities ultimately cool the body's core temperature.

Hantavirus Pulmonary Syndrome (HPS). Deer mice spread the virus that causes HPS, and humans contract it from breathing it in, usually when they've disturbed an area with dust and mice feces from nests or surfaces with mice droppings or urine. Exposure to large numbers of rodents and their feces or urine presents the greatest risk. As hikers, we sometimes enter old buildings, and often deer mice live in these places. We may not be around long enough to be exposed, but do be aware of this disease. About half the people who develop HPS die. Symptoms are flu-like and appear about two to three weeks after exposure. After initial symptoms, a dry cough and shortness of breath follow. Breathing is difficult. If you even think you might have HPS, see a doctor immediately!

Preparedness

It's been said that failing to plan means planning to fail. So do take the necessary time to plan your trip. Whether going on a short or an extended camping trip, always prepare for the worst. Simply remembering to pack a copy of the U.S. Army Survival Manual is not preparedness. Although it's not a bad idea if you plan on entering truly wild places, it's merely the tourniquet answer to a problem. You need to do your best to prevent the problem from arising in the first place. In order to survive—and to stay reasonably comfortable—you need to concern yourself with the basics: water, food, and shelter. Don't camp without having these bases covered. And don't go camping expecting to find these items in the woods.

Water. Even in frigid conditions, you need at least two quarts of water a day to function efficiently. Add heat and taxing terrain and you can bump that figure up to one gallon. That's simply a base to work from—your metabolism and your level of conditioning can raise or lower that amount. Unless you know your level, assume that you need one gallon of water a day. Now, where do you plan on getting the water?

Preferably not from natural water sources. These sources can be loaded with intestinal disturbers, such as bacteria, viruses, and fertilizers. *Giardia lamblia*, the most common of these disturbers, is a protozoan parasite that lives part of its life cycle as a cyst in water sources. The parasite spreads when mammals defecate in water sources. Once ingested, Giardia can induce cramping, diarrhea, vomiting, and fatigue within two days to two weeks after ingestion. Giardiasis is treatable with prescription drugs. If you believe you've contracted giardiasis, see a doctor immediately.

Treating water. The best and easiest solution to avoid polluted water is to carry your water with you. Yet, depending on the nature of your camping trip and the duration, this may not be an option—one gallon of water weighs eight-and-a-half pounds. In that case, you'll need to look into treating water. Regardless of which method you choose, you should always carry some water with you in case of an emergency. Save this reserve until you absolutely need it.

There are three methods of treating water: boiling, chemical treatment, and filtering. If you boil water, it's recommended that you do so for ten to fifteen minutes. This is often impractical because you're forced to exhaust a great deal of your fuel supply. You can opt for chemical treatment, which will kill Giardia but will not take care of other chemical pollutants. Another drawback to chemical treatments is the unpleasant taste of the water after it's treated. You can remedy this by adding powdered drink mix to the water. Filters are the preferred method for treating water. Many filters remove Giardia, organic and inorganic contaminants, and don't leave an aftertaste. Water filters are far from perfect as they can easily become clogged or leak if a gasket wears out. It's always a good idea to carry a backup supply of chemical treatment tablets in case your filter decides to quit on you.

Food. If we're talking about survival, you can go days without food, as long as you have water. But we're also talking about comfort. Try to avoid foods that are high in sugar and fat like candy bars and potato chips. These food types are harder to digest and are low in nutritional value. Instead, bring along foods that are easy to pack, nutritious, and high in energy (e.g., bagels, nutrition bars, dehydrated fruit, gorp, and jerky). When on an overnight trip, easy-to-fix dinners include rice mixes with dehydrated potatoes, corn, pasta with cheese sauce, and soup mixes. For a tasty breakfast, you can fix hot oatmeal with brown sugar and reconstituted milk powder topped off with banana chips. If you like a hot drink in the morning, bring along herbal tea bags or hot chocolate. If you are a coffee junkie, you can purchase coffee that is packaged like tea bags. You can prepackage all of your meals in heavy-duty resealable plastic bags to keep food from spilling in your pack. These bags can be reused to pack out trash.

Shelter. The type of shelter you choose depends less on the conditions than on your tolerance for discomfort. Shelter comes in many forms—tent, tarp, lean-to, bivy sack, cabin, cave, etc. If you're camping in the desert, a bivy sack may suffice, but if you're above the treeline and a storm is approaching, a better choice is a three- or four-season tent. Tents are the logical and most popular choice for most backpackers as they're lightweight and packable—and you can rest assured that you always have shelter from the elements. Before you leave on your trip, anticipate what the weather and terrain will be like and plan for the type of shelter that will work best for your comfort level (see Equipment later in this section).

Finding a campsite. If there are established campsites, stick to those. If not, start looking for a campsite early—around 3:30 or 4:00 p.m. Stop at the first decent site you see. Depending on the area, it could be a long time before you find another suitable location. Pitch your camp in an area that's level. Make sure the area is at least 200 feet from fragile areas like lakeshores, meadows, and stream banks. And try to avoid areas thick in underbrush, as they can harbor insects and provide cover for approaching animals.

If you are camping in stormy, rainy weather, look for a rock outcrop or a shelter in the trees to keep the wind from blowing your tent all night. Be sure that you don't camp under trees with dead limbs that might break off on top of you. Also, try to find an area that has an absorbent surface, such as sandy soil or forest duff. This, in addition to camping on a surface with a slight angle, will provide better drainage. By all means, don't dig trenches to provide drainage around your tent—remember you're practicing zero-impact camping.

If you're in bear country, steer clear of creekbeds or animal paths. If you see any signs of a bear's presence (i.e., scat, footprints), relocate. You'll need to find a campsite near a tall tree where you can hang your food and other items that may attract bears such as deodorant, toothpaste, or soap. Carry a lightweight nylon rope with which to hang your food. As a rule, you should hang your food at least 20 feet from the ground and 5 feet away from the tree trunk. You can put food and other items in a waterproof stuff sack and tie one end of the rope to the stuff sack. To get the other end of the rope over the tree branch, tie a good size rock to it, and gently toss the rock over the tree branch. Pull the stuff sack up until it reaches the top of the branch and tie it off securely. Don't hang your food near your tent! If possible, hang your food at least 100 feet away from your campsite. Alternatives to hanging your food are bear-proof plastic tubes and metal bear boxes.

Lastly, think of comfort. Lie down on the ground where you intend to sleep and see if it's a good fit. For morning warmth (and a nice view to wake up to), have your tent face east.

Natural Hazards

Besides tripping over a rock or tree root on the trail, there are some real hazards to be aware of while camping. Even if where you're camping doesn't have the plethora of poisonous snakes and plants, insects, and grizzly bears found in other parts of the United States, there are a few weather conditions and predators you may need to take into account.

Lightning. Thunderstorms build over the mountains almost every day during the summer. Lightning is generated by thunderheads and can strike without warning, even several miles away from the nearest overhead cloud. The best rule of thumb is to start leaving exposed peaks, ridges, and canyon rims by about noon. This time can vary a little depending on storm buildup. Keep an eye on cloud formation and don't underestimate how fast a storm can build. The bigger they get, the more likely a thunderstorm will happen. Lightning takes the path of least resistance, so if you're the high point, it might choose you. Ducking under a rock overhang is dangerous as you form the shortest path between the rock and ground. If you dash below treeline, avoid standing under the only or the tallest tree. If you are caught above treeline, stay away from anything metal you might be carrying, Move down off the ridge slightly to a low, treeless point and squat until the storm passes. If you have an insulating pad, squat on it. Avoid having both your hands and feet touching the ground at once and never lay flat. If you hear a buzzing sound or feel your hair standing on end, move quickly as an electrical charge is building up.

Flash floods. On July 31, 1976, a torrential downpour unleashed by a thunderstorm dumped tons of water into the Big Thompson watershed near Estes Park. Within hours, a wall of water moved down the narrow canyon killing 139 people and causing more than $30 million in property damage. The spooky thing about flash floods, especially in western canyons, is that they can appear out of nowhere from a storm many miles away. While camping or driving in canyons, keep an eye on the weather. Always climb to safety if danger threatens. Flash floods usually subside quickly, so be patient and don't cross a swollen stream.

Bears. Most of the United States (outside of the Pacific Northwest and parts of the Northern Rockies) does not have a grizzly bear population, although some rumors exist about sightings where there should be none. Black bears are plentiful, however. Here are some tips in case you and a bear scare each other. Most of all, avoid scaring a bear. Watch for bear tracks (five toes) and droppings (sizable with leaves, partly digested berries, seeds, and/or animal fur). Talk or sing where visibility or hearing are limited. Keep a clean camp, hang food, and don't sleep in the clothes you wore while cooking. Be especially careful in spring to avoid getting between a mother and her cubs. In late summer and fall bears are busy eating berries and acorns to fatten up for winter, so be extra careful around berry bushes and oakbrush. If you do encounter a bear, move away slowly while facing the bear, talk softly, and avoid direct eye contact. Give the bear room to escape. Since bears are very curious, it might stand upright to get a better whiff of you, and it may even charge you to try to intimidate you. Try to stay calm. If a bear does attack you, fight back with anything you have handy. Unleashed dogs have been known to come running back to their owners with a bear close behind. Keep your dog on a leash or leave it at home.

Mountain lions. Mountain lions appear to be getting more comfortable around humans as long as deer (their favorite prey) are in an area with adequate cover. Usually elusive and quiet, lions rarely attack people. If you meet a lion, give it a chance to escape. Stay calm and talk firmly to it. Back away slowly while facing the lion. If you run, you'll only encourage the curious cat to chase you. Make yourself look large by opening a jacket, if you have one, or waving your hiking poles. If the lion behaves aggressively throw stones, sticks, or whatever you can while remaining tall. If a lion does attack, fight for your life with anything you can grab. Moose. Because moose have very few natural predators, they don't fear humans like other animals. You might find moose in sagebrush and wetter areas of willow, aspen, and pine, or in beaver habitats. Mothers with calves, as well as bulls during mating season, can be particularly aggressive. If a moose threatens you, back away slowly and talk calmly to it. Keep your pets away from moose.

Other considerations. Hunting is a popular sport in the United States, especially during rifle season in October and November. Camping is still enjoyable in those months in many areas, so just take a few precautions. First, learn when the different hunting seasons start and end in the area in which you'll be camping. During this time frame, be sure to wear at least a blaze orange hat, and possibly put an orange vest over your pack. Don't be surprised to see hunters in camo outfits carrying bows or muzzleloading rifles around during their season. If you would feel more comfortable without hunters around, camp in national parks and monuments or state and local parks where hunting is not allowed.

Camping with Children

Camping with children isn't a matter of how many miles you can cover or how much elevation gain you make in a day; it's about seeing and experiencing nature through their eyes.

Kids like to explore and have fun. They like to stop and point out bugs and plants, look under rocks, jump in puddles, and throw sticks. If you're taking a toddler or young child on a hike, start with a trail that you're familiar with. Trails that have interesting things for kids, like piles of leaves to play in or a small stream to wade through during the summer, will make the hike much more enjoyable for them and will keep them from getting bored.

You can keep your child's attention if you have a strategy before starting on the trail. Using games is not only an effective way to keep a child's attention, it's also a great way to teach him or her about nature. Play hide and seek, where your child is the mouse and you are the hawk. Quiz children on the names of plants and animals. If your children are old enough, let them carry their own daypack filled with snacks and water. So that you are sure to go at their pace and not yours, let them lead the way. Playing follow the leader works particularly well when you have a group of children. Have each child take a turn at being the leader.

With children, a lot of clothing is key. The only thing predictable about weather is that it will change. Especially in mountainous areas, weather can change dramatically in a very short time. Always bring extra clothing for children, regardless of the season. In the winter, have your children wear wool socks, and warm layers such as long underwear, a fleece jacket and hat, wool mittens, and good rain gear. It's not a bad idea to have these along in late fall and early spring as well. Good footwear is also important. A sturdy pair of high top tennis shoes or lightweight hiking boots are the best bet for little ones. If you're camping in the summer near a lake or stream, bring along a pair of old sneakers that your child can put on when he wants to go exploring in the water. Remember when you're near any type of water, always watch your child at all times. Also, keep a close eye on teething toddlers who may decide a rock or leaf of poison oak is an interesting item to put in their mouth.

From spring through fall, you'll want your kids to wear a wide-brimmed hat to keep their face, head, and ears protected from the hot sun. Also, make sure your children wear sunscreen at all times. Choose a brand without Paba—children have sensitive skin and may have an allergic reaction to sunscreen that contains Paba. If you are camping with a child younger than six months, don't use sunscreen or insect repellent. Instead, be sure that their head, face, neck, and ears are protected from the sun with a wide-brimmed hat, and that all other skin exposed to the sun is protected with the appropriate clothing.

Remember that food is fun. Kids like snacks so it's important to bring a lot of munchies for the trail. Stopping often for snack breaks is a fun way to keep the trail interesting. Raisins, apples, granola bars, crackers and cheese, cereal, and trail mix all make great snacks. If your child is old enough to carry her own backpack, fill it with treats before you leave. If your kids don't like drinking water, you can bring boxes of fruit juice.

Avoid poorly designed child-carrying packs—you don't want to break your back carrying your child. Most child-carrying backpacks designed to hold a forty-pound child will contain a large carrying pocket to hold diapers and other items. Some have an optional rain/sun hood.

Index

About the Author

Tom Behrens has camped for more than fifty years in different parts of the United States. Born in Cincinnati, Ohio, he moved to Texas in 1976, and since then he has camped, explored, fished, and hunted throughout the state. He and his wife, Ann, live in Katy, Texas.

WHAT'S SO SPECIAL ABOUT UNSPOILED, NATURAL PLACES?

Beauty   Solitude   Wildness   Freedom   Quiet   Adventure

Serenity   Inspiration   Wonder   Excitement

Relaxation   Challenge

There's a lot to love about our treasured public lands, and the reasons are different for each of us. Whatever your reasons are, the national **Leave No Trace** education program will help you discover special outdoor places, enjoy them, and preserve them—today and for those who follow. By practicing and passing along these simple principles, you can help protect the special places you love from being loved to death.

THE PRINCIPLES OF **LEAVE NO TRACE**

- Plan ahead and prepare
- Travel and camp on durable surfaces
- Dispose of waste properly
- Leave what you find
- Minimize campfire impacts
- Respect wildlife
- Be considerate of other visitors

Leave No Trace is a national nonprofit organization dedicated to teaching responsible outdoor recreation skills and ethics to everyone who enjoys spending time outdoors.

To learn more or to become a member, please visit us at www.LNT.org or call (800) 332–4100.

Leave No Trace, P.O. Box 997, Boulder, CO 80306

Visit the premier outdoor online community .

FALCON GUIDES®

LOGIN | CREATE AN ACCOUNT

Search

4 of 6

The Art of Cycling
Bicycling In Traffic
Part one: Beyond the Vehicular Cycling Principle

HIKING WITH KIDS

HAPPY TRAILS Hiking in the Great Outdoors is a simple gift we all can give our children, grandchildren, and young friends. Unlike playing music, writing poetry, painting pictures, or other activities that also can fill your soul, hiking does not require any special skill. All you need to do is put one foot in front of the other in the outdoors, repeatedly. And breathe deeply.

⊕ **LEARN MORE**

FEATURED NEW BOOK

SCAVENGER HIKE ADVENTURES: GREAT SMOKY MOUNTAINS NATIONAL PARK

A Totally New Interactive Hiking Guide

Introducing a brand new genre of hiking guide. Readers follow clues to find over 200 hidden natural and historic treasures on as many as 14 easy, moderate, and extreme hikes national parks. Follow the clues and find such things as a tree clawed open by a bear searching for food, an ancient Indian footpath, the remains of an old Model T Ford deep in the forest, and over 200 other unusual treasures.

⊕ CLICK HERE TO FIND OUT MORE

RECENT BLOG POSTS

- A Dry River
- Stat-mongering -- Look Out!
- Lizard Man
- Tropical Tip of Texas
- Lions And Snakes and Bears...Oh My! "Don's PCT Update"
- Bikin' in C'ville
- The Red Store
- Journey to Idyllwild
- A Spring Quandary
- Whew!! Rocky Mountain book is printed I'm going camping!!

more

EXPERT BLOGS

- Arrow leaf Balsamroot—Another
  By: Bert Gildart
- Splitter camps #2
  By: Katie Brown
- Splitter camp
  By: Katie Brown
- Alaska Boating A...

outfit your mind®

- Chris Sharma
- Beth Rodden
- Dean Potter
- Jason Kehl
- Josh Wharton
- Steph Davis

falcon.com

Lightning Source UK Ltd.
Milton Keynes UK
UKHW011152141019
351577UK00005B/1280/P